Getting Started *with* HANDPLANES

How to Choose, Set Up, and Use Planes for Fantastic Results

——— Scott Wynn ———

ACKNOWLEDGMENTS

To my father, Jerry, who taught me always to watch and listen; and to my daughter, Josephine, who stands on her grandfather's shoulders watching, listening, and learning—and teaching all of us.

I would also like to acknowledge the untiring support of my partner Kathy Tam and the helpful guidance of technical editor Rick Mastelli, which made this book possible.

All illustrations by Scott Wynn.

Photos by Rick Mastelli, Scott Wynn, and Jon Deck.

© 2017 by Scott Wynn and Fox Chapel Publishing Company, Inc., East Petersburg, PA.

Getting Started with Handplanes is a revised and expanded edition of material in *Woodworker's Guide to Handplanes* (2010). This version is published in 2017 by Fox Chapel Publishing Company, Inc.

ISBN 978-1-56523-885-5

Library of Congress Cataloging-in-Publication Data

Names: Wynn, Scott, author.
Title: Getting started with handplanes / Scott Wynn.
Description: Petersburg, PA : Fox Chapel Publishing Company, Inc., [2017] |
   Includes index.
Identifiers: LCCN 2016046034 | ISBN 9781565238855
Subjects: LCSH: Planes (Hand tools) | Woodwork.
Classification: LCC TT186 .W96 2017 | DDC 684/.082--dc23
LC record available at https://lccn.loc.gov/2016046034

To learn more about the other great books from Fox Chapel Publishing, or to find a retailer near you,
call toll-free 800-457-9112 or visit us at *www.FoxChapelPublishing.com*.

Note to Authors: We are always looking for talented authors to write new books. Please send a brief letter
describing your idea to Acquisitions Editor, 1970 Broad Street, East Petersburg, PA 17520.

Printed in Singapore
First printing

GETTING STARTED *with* HANDPLANES

How to Choose, Set Up, and Use Planes for Fantastic Results

—— Scott Wynn ——

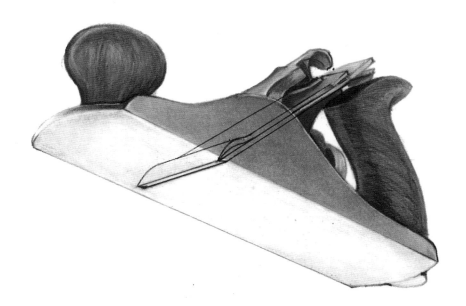

FOX CHAPEL
PUBLISHING

CONTENTS

CHAPTER 8: SHARPENING PLANE BLADES

CHAPTER 9: BENCH WORK

CHAPTER 10: MAKING & USING SHOOTING BOARDS

INTRODUCTION

I cannot think of anyone who has made a shaving with a plane and not been seduced by the sight, sound, and feel of the shaving emerging from the top. It is a tool of enormous satisfaction. However, it is far more than the pleasure of using a plane that makes it important. The handplane quickly and effectively does things other tools cannot. Power tools have redefined and often supplanted the handplane's traditional role, but have not replaced it. Understanding the handplane (how to set it up, fine-tune it, and adjust and modify its anatomy) and the variety of jobs it handles increases options for work and efficiency and improves results, allowing you to experience the satisfaction this essential tool brings.

The Pleasures of Handplanes

A machine might best accomplish a repeated task (you decide how many justifies automation), but hand tools can efficiently assist or accomplish short runs, one-of-a-kind pieces, prototypes, and variations on a theme. I find one of the main advantages to a proficiency with hand tools is fewer limitations in the types of projects I am able to tackle—projects otherwise too small or too big, projects too complex, and projects whose form is evolving even as they're being produced. Even if you are working in production or large millwork situations, handplane skills can be a godsend.

In addition to extending the range of projects you can tackle, the handplane is demonstrably faster for some tasks, including smoothing small parts. A well-set handplane can smooth a side of a leg, for instance, smoother than 1,000-grit sandpaper in two or three strokes, with none of the rounding or waviness you might get with sanding. A few strokes of a handplane can likewise remove the saw marks and tearing you get on end grain. A follow-up of a few strokes with 220-grit sandpaper and you get quick, baby-bottom smoothness. The best tool to remove snipe and power-planer variations is the handplane, as its flat sole flattens the board in removing the snipe. It is fast, and it is accurate.

The results you get with a handplane are different from those with sandpaper. Assuming the blade is correctly shaped, a handplaned piece is going to be flatter and straighter than all but the work produced with the best wide-belt sanders. Less expensive wide-belt sanders can leave ripples similar to a planer. Belt and orbit sanders

leave a gently wavy surface like calm water that shows up especially after applying finish, on horizontal surfaces. If you have a flat-grain piece, say in oak or pine, sanding removes more softer spring growth than denser late-season growth, resulting in a gently rippling surface following the grain. This will not happen with a handplane. Power sanding, particularly with the random-orbit sander, tends to slightly round over work in general, but especially smaller pieces, sometimes giving the work a doughy look. Handplaning also provides a better surface for gluing.

Besides the difference in surface quality, there is a subtle but palpable difference in the look and character between pieces shaped and smoothed by edge tools and those prepared by sanding. The crispness and flow suggestive of the sweep of the cutting edge is not present in work abraded to shape. That is an important and critical lesson for woodworkers. This is not to say one or another piece would be inferior, but there are differences in the look and feel of the piece. Understanding the difference helps you choose the correct tool.

Your Health Concerns

Also important to consider in the choice between power tools and handplanes is exposure to dust. Long underestimated, the dangers of dust are now becoming more apparent. The U.S. government has officially identified wood dust as a carcinogen. The modern production shop produces large quantities of it. The one-man shop, with its orbital, belt, stationary, spindle, disk, and thickness sanders can produce choking amounts of it. The widespread use of abrasives is relatively new, so the long-term effects of dust inhalation are not fully known, nor are the effects of the many compounds in wood—many of them toxic, allergenic or simply irritating. These include those associated with any rot-resistant wood and many tropical hardwoods. We know they can cause rashes and other skin reactions. Particles inhaled deeply into the lungs can cause permanent lung damage. The smallest dust particles, which sanding produces, are the most dangerous. Some particles are so small they pass through the best filters. Read the product specifications—no filtration system, no dust mask is 100% effective. A dust collector can actually make things worse. Anything not collected by the filter (particles from 30 microns to less than 1 micron, depending on your filter) will be blown back into the air, continually suspended, and circulated by the collector until you turn it off. Even if the filtration material in a dust mask were better, no dust mask fit is airtight, especially if worn over a beard.

Concern extends beyond the lungs. Long-term dust exposure can cause nasal polyps, which can be pre-cancerous. There also is the very real risk of hearing loss from machine noise. Many woodworkers I know who are my age have suffered some hearing loss.

Therefore, woodworkers should approach sanding with more awareness, and take steps to limit and control their exposure to dust and noise. They should also consider methods beyond a sander for achieving a shape or surface. Perhaps the image of the woodworker quietly planing wood, listening for the sound of a well cut shaving, the floor littered with (dust-free) streams of shavings, and the bench and tools so free of dust you could wear black clothes to work and leave without a mark is less romantic and more serious than it would seem. It certainly represents a better quality of life than standing over a screaming, dust-spewing sander for hours on end.

Your Wallet

And what about the economics? The handplane can be more cost-effective than sandpaper. Look at the costs of a random-orbit sander. You have the initial investment, less probably than for a good plane, but not cheap. You have the cost of sandpaper: use the sander all day long and you can easily burn through $20 to $30 worth of sandpaper. Three or four days of that and you just bought yourself a handplane. You have downtime when the machine is sidelined for repairs. You are not going to be doing any sanding with it, and when you are not sanding with it, you are not making money. Then there is the cost of repairs: replace the bearings, brushes, and hook-and-loop pad (which also wears out), and you have just about bought yourself another sander. In addition, no matter what, eventually the machine wears out and must be replaced. If you were to use a random orbit sander every day, all day, you would wear it out in a year after having the machine repaired twice. Use a handplane all day, every day, and you have worn maybe a half-inch off the blade. You would be able to get another two maybe three years out of that $40 blade. Assuming you make the correct decisions as to the appropriate tool to use as you work, the *efficiency* of each tool becomes equal, but the *cost* of the sander is many times higher.

There are, of course, costs associated with the handplane, but they compare favorably. Once you have set the plane up, maintenance is minimal. Sharpening can be a pain, but with some practice and decent technique, you can be back to work in five minutes or less, depending on the type of plane. The learning curve for the handplane is higher, but woodworking requires the continual acquisition and advancement of skill. That is the essence of the craft. You do not have to leap into the most challenging uses of the plane right at the beginning. Expand your handplane skills gradually as your skill progresses. The information in this book will greatly shorten the learning curve.

Abrasives are here to stay and will continue to be an important part of woodworking. To not use all of the skills and techniques available or to not acquire the knowledge that will help you choose the appropriate technique, and the skill to follow through, limits the scope of your work, your creativity, and growth.

Rewards

Knowledgeable use of both power and hand tools leads to better, more rewarding work, and the handplane, always the premier woodworking instrument, remains one of the most useful tools available. By temperament, and perhaps because of how you see your pieces, you will naturally favor hand tools over power tools, or vice versa, but it is important you make a reasoned decision. The first step to understanding the effectiveness of a technology—in this case woodworking handplanes—is to fully understand the capabilities and limitations of the tool. That is what this book aims to accomplish.

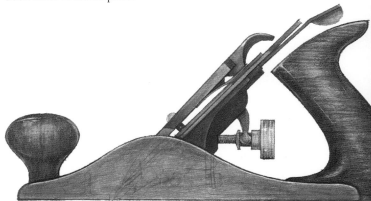

1

SMOOTH
What to Use, When, and Why

Different tools leave different surfaces, discernable by eye, hand, or both. While the differences may be subtle, they still are often immediately recognizable. End users, in particular, can respond quite strongly, even without fully understanding why. Such subtle differences distinguish craftwork from production work and make it sought out by potential buyers, whether consciously or not, and can literally close the sale.

The handplane is unmatched in its ability to get a crisp, clean, clear surface on wood.

Figure 1-1.
The grit in sandpaper acts like a series of minute pointed scrapers, removing wood by compression failure at the points of the abrasive. It is a reliable way to smooth wood, but in some ways it's like using an uneven bed of nails: it leaves a series of erratic uneven grooves across the board, often leaves little balls of wood fiber at the end of the grooves, and tears the edges of the wood pores and fills them with dust. Clarity of the woods grain and figure is compromised for reliability.

To get to that level of finesse—of craftsmanship—the use, position, and intended finish of a piece, or parts of a piece, all have to be considered when deciding on the best tools to use for a project. To make informed decisions, understanding the nature of the different surfaces different tools produce is essential.

The three ways to smooth wood—sanding, scraping, and planing—all leave a different kind of surface.

SANDING

Sanding abrades the surface, leaving a series of irregular microscopic grooves with slightly fuzzy edges. Sandpaper, which consists of randomly distributed abrasive particles of irregular size, shape, and orientation, tears and scrapes the wood fibers. The points and edges of the particles project and wear unevenly, cutting

to different depths. The result is most noticeable when starting with coarse sandpaper and then skipping grits, because coarser grits leave deep scratches finer grits will not reach (Figure 1-1). Sanding also leaves a myriad of microscopic torn fibers hanging onto the surface. And even though you may be meticulous, sanding thoroughly through progressive grits, you still have to sand to a grit finer than 600 to get light to penetrate through the torn fibers with enough clarity to bring out the grain of a figured wood.

SCRAPING

Scraping, using the burr turned on the edge of a sharpened blade held at a high angle, tears the wood fibers as well, removing wood essentially by compression failure at the edge of the burr (Figure 1-2). The burr is a relatively blunt cutting edge that establishes a point where compression failure begins, rather than actually cutting or shearing the wood. Hard tropical woods scrape cleanly, I suppose, because scoring the wood fibers with a blunt edge is more effective on hard, brittle wood. But the softer the species, the less cleanly the burr-edge pulls wood away, often causing the chip to collapse upon itself, while tearing the fibers from the surface being smoothed. A scraper shapes the surface of pine, for instance, but it ends up fuzzy.

The big advantage the scraper has over sandpaper is that on most hardwoods, it removes wood as fast as 60-grit paper and leaves a finish like 400-grit, all with one tool that will probably last a lifetime and costs the same as a single package of sandpaper. Moreover, unlike a plane, it is virtually impossible to get any major tearout with a scraper, though on some woods, the resulting fuzziness confirms surface tears. Nor is the scraper unidirectional, as some believe. It cuts better in one direction than the other, though cutting in the wrong direction does not usually result in the disastrous tearout you might get with a plane.

Both sanding and scraping leave the edges of the wood pores ragged, though technically the results are slightly different. With sanding, the last grit used determines the size of the ragged fibers. Whatever the grit, however, torn fibers are plentiful. (See Figure 1-3.) With scraping, the ragged fibers are fewer and longer. In both cases, the fibers lie flat until finish is applied, and then stand up, swollen and stiffened with the finish.

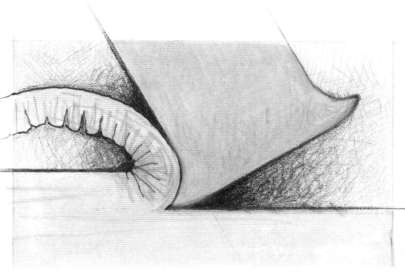

Figure 1-2. *A cabinet scraper removes wood by compression failure parallel to the grain at the edge of the burr. While it can give dependable results, a heavy cut can result in erratic failure both in front of and below the edge, snowpiling the chip and reducing the quality of the surface. Making a light cut attains best results.*

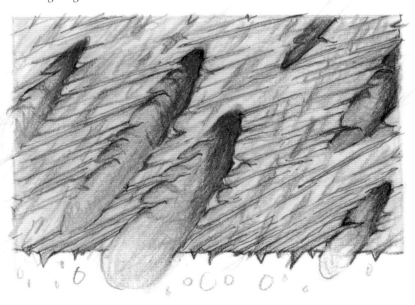

Figure 1-3. *Deep scratches and torn fibers characterize the sanded wood surface. Sanding tears fibers in the surface of wood, while scraping leaves behind fewer ragged fibers that tend to be longer.*

PLANING

A sharpened plane cuts by shearing the fibers off cleanly. The lower the angle of the cut, the cleaner the shear; the higher the angle, the more the blade scrapes. The shearing cut is clean—the surface is not torn by abrasion

Figure 1-4.
A handplane removes wood by shearing the fibers right at the point of its thin, sharp edge. Though the results can be less dependable (unless the cut is controlled by the methods described in Chapter 3), the remaining surface is not torn by abrasion or compression failure, revealing the beauty of the wood's grain and figure.

or compression failure—and light penetrates the surface structure, refracting through the changes in direction of the wood grain, and revealing the dazzling beauty of the wood's figure. (See Figure 1-4.)

However, in the practical, day-to-day world, even this surface deserves further consideration. Most woods show wonderful clarity with a little raggedness remaining at the end of the pores—a kind of tail or thin fringe to an otherwise cleanly cut pore. (See Figure 1-5.) This residue rises when applying finish and stiffens when the finish dries, resulting in a surface that feels slightly rough. Removing the tails to achieve a smooth surface results in a conundrum: in order to get the smoothest surface you must risk compromising clarity by lightly roughing it up.

ADDING FINISH

There are a couple of ways to approach the ·issue. The first is to consider the proposed

finish. *Penetrating finishes,* such as oil, raise the grain less and bring out the figure of the grain more than surface finishes. On some woods, vigorous application and removal of the oil with a rag eliminates them, especially if the last step is to buff with a wool rag.

Some woods require rubbing with steel wool after the first or second coat of oil. Steel wool hooks the hanging fibers and pulls them off, burnishing, more than abrading,

Figure 1-5. *Scraping often leaves a tail at the end of the wood pore the length of which varies from species to species. Planing also can sometimes result in a tail depending on the species, but it is usually much smaller. A coat of finish raises and stiffens the tails and other irregularities, making the surface look and feel rough.*

the surface. You can polish some surfaces by rubbing them hard with leftover shavings before applying oil. This method works particularly well with smaller parts, such as legs and stretchers. It is less successful on broad surfaces, especially horizontal ones, as the burnishing tends to be uneven.

I usually go over broad and/or horizontal surfaces after planing, when using oil as a finish, with a very fine grit of sandpaper. If I did a particularly good job on softwood, for instance, I may polish the surface with 1000 grit or finer—or if it looks really good, I may wait until I give it a coat of oil and see if any roughness appears, which I will then remove with 1000+ sandpaper.

On hardwood, especially if I expect to give the surface numerous coats of oil, I may sand first with 400 to 600 grit, depending on how even I was able to plane the surface. After several coats, I'll sand with 600 to 800 grit and apply more coats. Vertical surfaces don't need this type of attention; sanding with 400 grit or 0000 steel wool after two or three coats of oil, followed by another coat or two, is sufficient.

Surface finishes, such as varnish or lacquer, do not bring out the figure as well as oil for two reasons: (1) the finish does not penetrate as deeply and (2) light must travel through a thickness of film before striking the wood and bouncing back through again. The clean shear you get from planing is muted, and therefore probably less critical. I have also had feedback from finishers that (in one case anyway) the plane left the surface too smooth without enough tooth for the finish to adhere.

To prepare for a heavy surface finish, such as brushed varnish, catalyzed varnish and lacquer, or nitrocellulose lacquer, my general procedure is to remove the machining marks, snipe, and such with a plane. If the plane leaves minor tearout, I remove it with a card scraper. If the project or parts of it (like shelving) are less sensitive—and especially if the wood is difficult—I may remove the mill marks with a handled scraper, such as the Stanley #80, followed by the card scraper.

A handled scraper is much faster than sanding through three or four grits of sandpaper. I follow the planing (or scraping) with a quick, light pass with 220-grit sandpaper to even out any minor irregularities or any traces of the plane or scraper. If the finish is to be shellac, I will follow the planing (and scraping if necessary) with 320- or 400-grit sandpaper (except for French polishing, which has its own set of procedures).

Shellac does not seem to flow out as well as lacquer, even when applied thickly or repeatedly, and seems to benefit from extra sanding. The catalyzed finishes flow out wonderfully and cover a multitude of sins. Unfortunately, they can also make a closed-pore wood like cherry look like plastic laminate.

FLAT AND SMOOTH

On broad horizontal surfaces, take special care to prepare the surface, no matter what the finish. Once the light glances across the surface, variations in flatness will literally be glaring. Sanding a horizontal surface flat will not yield satisfactory results. Belt sanders and orbital sanders used directly after power planing will result in a surface that looks like a calm pond in a slight breeze when the light reflects across it. I have found most stationary thickness sanders do not give satisfactory results, either. Only the top-end industrial sanders used to finish plywood sheets give anything close to acceptable results.

Hand planing yields flat surfaces, especially if the handplanes used are the correct size for the work. Unfortunately, large surface handplaning is one of the hardest skills to master, though the results can be quite rewarding. Using the tools, techniques, and information presented in this book can accelerate your efforts to acquire these skills. Flattening and smoothing a horizontal surface requires a series of handplanes. If tearout or minor imperfections remain, follow with one or two scrapers. Use a handled scraper, such as a scraping plane (not the Stanley #80) to maintain flatness if tearout is extensive. Use a card scraper over the whole surface for minor tearout. Usually this leaves the surface sufficiently flat and smooth so that, depending on the finish, a light sanding with 220-grit or finer is all that is needed. Often I can even skip this step and have to sand only lightly after the sealer coat of finish.

If I am not satisfied that planing and scraping have left the surface sufficiently flat, I may sand using 220-grit or finer with a half-sheet sanding block to remove any of the very slight ridges or any minor unevenness left between the cuts of the plane or scraper. This way they will not telegraph through, either visually upon completion of the finish, or physically when sanding between coats. That is particularly important with a brushed-on varnish finish. The coats do not blend with each other but remain separate, so cutting through a coat will leave a ring, necessitating removal of the finish and starting over. (You can usually avoid cutting through to minor high spots, by either hand sanding without a block, or using a soft block, after the first coat of finish.)

THE CHALLENGE OF GRIT

The grit size on sandpaper refers to the *maximum size contained*. On most papers, up to 65% of the abrasive is smaller than the listed grit size, some quite a bit smaller. This means the scratch pattern will be inconsistent, with the listed grit size making deeper scratches than the remaining abrasive. This inconsistent scratch pattern will then have to be reduced by the inconsistent scratch pattern of the next finer grit, and so forth, until the scratch pattern is fine enough not to be easily discerned by the eye or hand. That is why you should not skip grades when sanding. Some of the new premium papers have a more consistent grit size with as much as 95% of the abrasive being of the listed size, so attaining good results should be easier.

HANDLING EDGES

There is another subtle difference that more than one client has pointed out to me. While the handplane leaves a surface whose visual and tactile quality usually is unsurpassed, the surface it leaves on an arris (a corner where two faces come together) usually can be improved. If you watch clients study pieces of furniture, they will always—consciously or not—run their hand along the edges of it, making the edges of a piece among its most important features. The edges can clinch the deal—or break it. Knocking the edges off with a handplane, no matter how finely done, will leave a somewhat harsh, unfriendly quality to the piece, even if done with a round-blade chamfer plane. Follow the final touches with a plane with a light sanding to soften the edges, usually with 220-grit sandpaper (or finer if the chamfer was well cut). This will make the all-important edges satisfying to the touch.

SUBTLE DIFFERENCES

So *smooth* is both visual and tactile, looking and feeling differently in different places, with different results from different tools, and sometimes different results with the same tools—in different woods. How do we use that information effectively in our day-to-day work? I have come to a number of conclusions through my experience working with planes. For one, removing a lot of wood by sanding is, in most situations, a poor and inefficient choice. Bring wood as closely as possible to its final shape and finish with a cutting edge—either a plane, scraper, or power tool. When the work is ground to shape with abrasives, the surface must be thoroughly sanded with each succeeding grit to ensure the deep scratches from the coarse shaping grit have been eliminated. This is expensive and time consuming, and raises excessive fine dust. Sandpaper's first use traditionally was as a final step in polishing the work, and at its most aggressive, removing minor tool marks. I think that remains its best use.

Another important point: Wood shaped by abrasives, rather than by a cutting edge, results in both the shape and surface being different. The differences are subtle, but important. Cut pieces reflect the crispness of the edge used to shape them, and the sweep of the stroke the artisan used to make the cut. Sanded pieces feel and look ground down, and reflect the back-and-forth scrubbing or rotary movement of the abrasives used. The artisan must be aware of the differences and how it will affect the final product.

In summary, on a piece where you want to bring out the figure and texture (grain) of the wood—a piece that is to have no finish or only a light finish (such as linseed, lemon, or tung oil), wax, or shellac—smoothing with a clean-cutting plane gives spectacular results and brings out the beauty of the wood. With some difficult-to-plane woods, however, taking the surface all of the way down to a polish with a plane can be demanding and not necessarily efficient. On some special pieces, the extra effort may be worth it. That is an individual decision. For most work, however, leveling with a plane, smoothing (if required) with a scraper, and a final polishing with sandpaper will be the most efficient procedure. This technique is especially applicable if a heavy surface finish such as lacquer, brushed varnish, or a catalyzed finish, is to be applied.

2

SHARP
The Cutting Edge

The blade is the heart of any plane. It may be held in place by exotic, expensive hardwood or marvelously machined bronze or iron, but it is the blade that does the work. If it is not up to the job, the plane becomes more of a curious decoration than a valued tool.

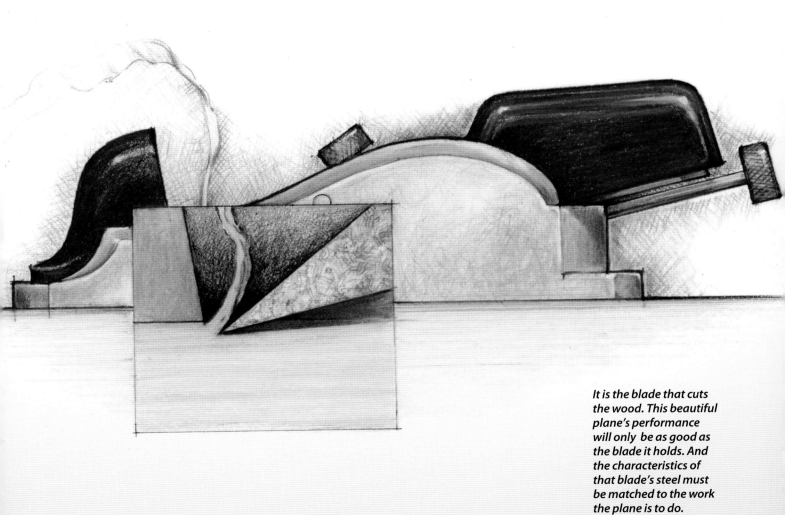

It is the blade that cuts the wood. This beautiful plane's performance will only be as good as the blade it holds. And the characteristics of that blade's steel must be matched to the work the plane is to do.

The claims tool manufacturers make about their blades are often confusing and contradictory, sometimes invoking near mystical qualities rather than offering real information. Sometimes the claims tout qualities applicable to industrial performance and are not meaningful to woodworkers. It was easier before: until around World War II the woodworker had little choice in the material for his blades—it would have been carbon steel. The only question was what quality he could afford. The purchase was often based on the manufacturer's reputation. Today, a wide variety of edge steel is available, with many industrial steels and processes being introduced and promoted as the next best thing. And to make matters worse, blade qualities are often subtle and can be hard to discern under many working conditions—until you start using it for the task it's not suited for.

Given such an overload of confusing information, it is tempting to ignore it, use the blade that comes with the plane, or buy the most expensive blade and hope price equals quality. Doing so ignores a critical link in the chain of knowledge required to do the best woodworking.

Steel is the interface between wood and woodworker, transmitting your concepts while shaping, smoothing, and transforming the wood. This interface—concentrated at the cutting edge—and the feedback it gives you, provides invaluable input affecting the finish,

fit, form, and feeling of the final product as it goes from concept to reality. Understanding the complexities of the steel used for the cutting edge helps you make decisions about the tools and techniques essential for effective, efficient work. This chapter clarifies some of these complexities.

While I know that for the woodworker, blade steel is not wood and is therefore of only indirect interest, having used a variety of blades over the years and having researched the results I was seeing in my day-to-day work, I have found that cutting edge steel is a delightfully complex subject, possessed of art and nuance. At first surmise, steel seems a simple material, cold and aloof. But though its qualities may be more subtle, its character more impenetrable than wood, its apparent coldness and aloofness can disguise great complexity. It becomes understandable that there is so much mystique surrounding the making of edge steel because, despite several hundred years of industry and science, the making of steel into blades for cutting wood remains an inexact science relying heavily on the experience, judgment, and skill of those involved in its production. Like the difference between a mass-produced piece of furniture and a fine handcrafted piece, a blade reveals to those who care to look the amount of effort put into its creation—be it a little or a lot. Like wood, steel has grain, structure, and movement. It can even have a bit of personality or a lack of it. Blade steel—especially forged blade steel—is alive with all of the energy the smith put into making it and the fire used to shape it. A woodworker should understand and appreciate the individuality of each blade, educate himself as he would with any of his tools, and apply this knowledge for greatest effect.

THE BASIC CRITERIA FOR A BLADE

The woodworker needs the edge on the hand tool blade to do three basic things: get sharp, stay sharp, and re-sharpen easily. These three qualities usually exist in balance with one another: increasing one probably decreases one or both of the others. In many applications, however, one quality may be most important, and the right blade choice depends upon understanding the strengths and weaknesses of the different steels—the balance each one strikes among these qualities.

There are additional considerations when selecting a blade, which I mention here and discuss in later chapters. The first consideration is the type of wood being cut. Softwoods and some softer hardwoods prefer an edge that is not only sharp but also *thin*. Only some steels can get really sharp, to a thinner bevel, and still hold an edge. As the wood gets harder, however, the steel's toughness becomes more important. Secondly, the edge requirements vary

according to the job. A blade required to remove a lot of wood—especially if it is hardwood or tropical hardwood—will need an edge that holds up well under the high heat build-up and impact that accompany vigorous use. The harder the wood, the more important the toughness of the steel.

Anatomy of Steel

The key to understanding edge steel is in its anatomy. I approach the anatomy of steel as a woodworker. The metallurgist or machinist will see things differently. For the needs of the woodworker, three characteristics define steel's anatomy—grain, structure, and hardness.

GRAIN

For woodworking hand tools, the grain of the steel is the most important characteristic

---

SHARPENING VERSUS RE-SHARPENING

I use *re-sharpen* here rather than *sharpen* or *sharpenability* because re-sharpen properly evokes the time and repetition involved that the others do not. I believe many woodworkers (myself included) do not keep their blades sharp enough, and I want to encourage them to change their habits. Many woodworkers believe sharpening is like cleaning the house: do it once and you are good for the week, or at least for the next few days. However, in reality, if you are using your plane all day, you will need to re-sharpen many times that day. Re-sharpening becomes the nuisance chore that keeps you from doing woodworking until it is done. *Easy* has a different meaning when it is done twenty times (or more) a week instead of just once.

of a blade. Ordered, repetitive arrangements of iron and alloy atoms in a crystalline structure comprise steel. The crystals can be small and fine or large and coarse. They can be consistent in size (evenly grained) or vary widely, with odd shapes and outsized clusters among the rest. The steel's grain affects how finely the blade sharpens and how quickly it dulls. Generally, the finer and more consistent the grain, the more finely it sharpens, the slower it dulls, and the better the blade performs.

Grain is a function of the initial quality of the steel used, the alloys added, and how the steel is worked or formed. In addition to the average size of the crystals, the initial quality of the steel may include impurities, called *inclusions*, which may persist throughout refining. Inclusions add large irregularities to the grain. Irregularities sometimes are used to good effect in swords and perhaps axes,

STEEL GRAIN

There is a standardized chart that refers to the average grain size within a steel. The numbers range from 00 to 14, with 00 being the largest (about ⅟₅₀"), and 14 the smallest (about ⅟₁₀,₀₀₀"). Manufacturers normally use fine grain size 7 or finer for the steel used in tools.

but except for the backing steel on laminated blades, impurities are a detriment to a plane blade. Sharpening impurities out to the edge causes them to break off easily, causing chipping and rapid dulling of the edge. The dirtier the steel, the more rapidly it dulls. Fine chipping will not affect the performance of an edge used for chopping wood; depending on the inclusion, it can add tensile,

shock-resisting strength to the blade. But for fine woodworking, such as planning a surface, even fine inclusions prevent sharpening the blade to its full potential, and shorten the edge's life.

Alloys change the texture of the grain. They may be part of the steel's original composition (though usually in small amounts), or added in a recipe to increase the steel's resistance to shock and heat. Alloys often coarsen the grain, so there is a trade-off. While the edge of an alloy blade may be more durable, especially under adverse working conditions, it may not sharpen as well as an unalloyed blade. To shear wood cleanly, no other attribute of an edge is more important than fineness.

STRUCTURE

Structure, the second most important aspect of a woodworking blade, is the result of the change that happens in the original composition of the steel due to heating it and changing its shape with a hammer (or rollers), often called *hot work*. Heat causes the crystals of the steel to grow. Hammering steel when it is hot causes its crystalline structures to fracture and impedes growth as the grains fracture into smaller crystals. Before being hot-worked, the crystals of steel are randomly oriented, and frequently inconsistent in size.

Through forging (repeatedly reshaping with a hammer while the steel is hot), the grain aligns and knits together in the direction of the metal flow. Proper forging increases grain structure consistency. When exposed at the edge through sharpening, crystals consistent in size and orientation break off one at a time as the blade dulls, rather than breaking off randomly in big clumps. The consistency of the crystals allows for a sharper blade that stays sharp longer.

The techniques used in preparing steel for woodworking tools are hammer forging, drop forging, and no forging. Hammer forging, where repeated hammer blows shape the steel, is the most desirable because it aligns the grain particles (or crystals) of the steel. It is a time-consuming, skillful process and therefore expensive. If improperly done, hammer forging stresses the steel, reducing rather than increasing reliability. With the general decline in hand-woodworking skills during the last century, and the increased reliance on power tools, the discriminating market that would appreciate the difference forging makes has shrunk considerably. As a result, hand-forged tools are not commonly manufactured or available in the United States.

Drop forging verges on die cutting. A large mechanized hammer called the punch drops on the heated blank, smashing it into a die (mold), giving the tool blade its rough shape, often in just one blow. For tools that vary considerably in cross-section, this method may be more desirable than grinding or cutting from stock, because the heat of grinding or cutting can cause some minor negative alteration in the grain structure at those areas. Drop forging imparts a marginally more consistent structure than a blade cut or ground from stock, because the

steel often elongates in the process, resulting in some improvement in the crystalline structure alignment.

Drop forging is preferable to no forging at all. No forging is an over-simplification because all tool steel receives some hot work during reshaping. Bar stock is hot-formed by rolling or extruding the ingot into lengths of consistent cross section. The process rearranges the crystalline structure and the crystals tend to align in the direction of the flow as the steel lengthens. However, the

THE IDEAL EDGE

The edge requirements for cutting different materials vary widely. The most obvious example is the edge required on a kitchen knife. Meat and vegetables are cut by the sawing action of drawing a coarse edge through them. A properly sharpened kitchen knife has what under a microscope would look like a series of small saw teeth, which result from sharpening it with an 800- or 1200-grit stone. If you are skeptical, sharpen your best kitchen knife with a #8000 stone and try to cut a potato. It will stop cutting halfway through and jam. While the knife is sharp enough to cut transparent shavings in wood, it will not cut halfway through a root vegetable. The lesson is that demonstrations of sharpness using other materials and claims of qualities originating in other trades and uses, such as industry or surgery, are not particularly useful in evaluating a woodworking blade.

Conceptually, for a blade to be perfect for woodworking, it must be possible to polish it down to single-crystal uniformity across its entire edge, with the crystals all lined up neatly, oriented the same direction, all very small and of the same size, equally hard, and tightly bonded to one another so they will not break off. In reality several types of crystals comprise a cutting edge. Crystals are greatly different in size and hardness and grouped together so they present themselves at the cutting edge in clusters, and so tend to break off in clusters, leaving voids and dull spots. The finest blades, however, have the qualities that enable something approaching the ideal edge.

arrangement is not very refined compared with the structure resulting when steel is hot-worked further at the forge. Modern Western chisel blades are frequently drop-forged (though some new premium chisels are being ground from A2 bar stock). Modern Western plane blades, even many after-market premium blades, are usually ground from unworked, rolled stock.

HARDNESS

Hardness is a major selling point in the advertising of woodworking tools made from various types of steel. However, as explained earlier, grain and structure are the most important factors in the performance of a blade. A plane blade soft enough to shape with a file (for instance, made from a piece of a good, old handsaw blade) will give excellent results if the fineness of its grain allows it to

DISSTON SAWS (AS DESCRIBED IN 'KEEPING THE CUTTING EDGE')

"...Disston saw steel was heat treated in the plant and was harder than competitive saws. We rolled our own saw sheets on a sheet mill so we could control the direction of grain within a sheet, enabling us to set the teeth at that hardness without their breaking. Disston saws were of a hardness that read 52–54 on the Rockwell C scale, and competitive saws were 46–48—about 10–15% softer than Disston's. They did not know the secret of how to roll a new saw sheet so the teeth would not break during setting at that hardness..."

From a letter written by Bill Disston, great-grandson of Henry Disston, to Harold Payson, as excerpted in Payson's book, *Keeping the Cutting Edge: Setting and Sharpening Hand and Power Saws* (Wooden Boat Books, 1988).

be sharpened well and its structure allows the edge to break off finely and evenly. I knew a boat builder who preferred plane blades made from good quality saw blades. The blades made it easy for him to file out nicks when his plane hit unexpected metal in the boat structure.

At the other end of the hardness spectrum is carbide, used on power tool blades. Hard and brittle, carbide is unsuitable for the body of the tool blade because it would shatter. While carbide is extremely hard, the particles are also extremely large. Although they do not break off easily, when they do, they break off in clumps so big they are nearly visible to the naked eye. Carbide also cannot be made nearly as sharp as steel. A sharp steel saw or router blade cuts much more cleanly than a sharp carbide blade. Unfortunately, the steel dulls quicker than the carbide, especially when subjected to the glues in plywood and particleboard.

Hardness must be in balance with the intended use of the tool. For instance, high-impact hand tools, such as axes, should be softer than plane blades. Otherwise, the edge fractures quickly under the pounding an ax takes. The blades of fine tools for fine work can be very hard, but if their hardness exceeds the ability of the steel to flex without breaking at the microscopic edge, the tool will be next to worthless.

The Rockwell C (Rc) scale measures the hardness of woodworking blades. This is a unit of measurement determined by the impact of a ball-shaped point into the steel measured in terms of the depth of the resulting impression. Japanese saws (harder than Western saws) are roughly in the 50–58 Rc range. This is on the cusp of what a file will cut. Decent plane and chisel blades are in the range of 58–66 Rc range—though I would expect a good quality plane blade to be at least Rc 60-62. Only some finely wrought steels work effectively in the upper-half of this range, principally high-quality hand-forged Japanese blades, and some high-alloy steels. In carbon steels, Rc 66 seems to be a limit above which the edge breaks down too rapidly in use, though I have heard of a Japanese master blacksmith who has made it a personal goal to develop steel that will hold an edge at about Rc 68. However, his experiments have not been available commercially.

In summary, grain, structure, and hardness are the characteristics of tool steel important to the woodworker using hand tools. Other tool users may emphasize other characteristics—primarily because they are working in other materials or using other methods. The cutting of wood fibers is a very particular application with very specific requirements. Only the right combination of grain, structure, and hardness—and method—provides good results.

HARDENING, TEMPERING, AND ANNEALING

The hardness and ductility (the extent to which it can be stretched or bent without breaking) of steel depends on its exact carbon-to-iron ratio and its thermal processing. Different temperatures are associated with different crystal structures, or phases, of the iron and carbon atoms. When steel with a carbon content above 0.4% (the minimum amount required for steel to harden) is heated beyond its critical temperature of around 750°C, it enters what is called the *austenite phase*. Austenite has a crystal structure that opens to allow the carbon atoms present to combine with the iron.

When austenite is cooled very quickly (by quenching) its structure changes to a needlelike crystalline form called *martensite*. Martensite locks in the carbon atom, *hardening* the steel. In this state the steel is at its hardest and is under a great deal of internal stress and quite brittle. The more carbon the steel had to begin with, the more of it will be martensite and the harder it will be. As the carbon goes over 0.8%, however, the steel does not become any harder but rather grows more brittle. In order for the steel to be useable as a blade, it must be softened to reduce the brittleness to a workable degree. The process is called *tempering*.

Tempering is a compromise, meant to balance hardness and ductility, and is definitely a judgment call made by the one doing the tempering, based both on experience and the intended use of the blade. To temper a blade, after hardening the blade is reheated, this time to a lower temperature (which depends on the type of steel and the blade's intended use), and quenched again.

There is a third process, done after the blade has been hot-worked to shape, but before hardening and tempering, and that is *annealing*. Here the blade is heated red hot and allowed to cool *without* quenching. This softens the blade and removes stresses that may have resulted from its being hot-worked. Usually at this point, the blade is then ground to final (or near final) shape—easily done, since it is now soft—and then hardened and finally tempered.

Types of Edge Steel

Steel for hand tool blades can be roughly divided into two categories: carbon steel and alloyed steel. All tool steels contain carbon, which makes it possible to harden the metal. Processed from iron and iron ore, carbon steel contains at least 0.5% carbon, and traces of other elements. Alloyed steel is carbon steel with small amounts of other elements added to improve performance under certain conditions and for certain purposes.

Manufacturers of steel have specific nomenclature and guidelines to the percentages of alloys used in each type of steel. Manufacturers of woodworking tools, however, have no such guidelines. The vast majority of Bailey planes made give little or no indication of the steel used. If they are marked, the manufacturer probably used a generic term for the steel that may encompass a group of dozens of different steels of widely varying recipes and characteristics. And while lately many hand tool manufacturers have been using the steel industries' nomenclature to indicate the steel they are using for their blades, this is by no means consistent. If you already have a plane and want to know what kind of steel the blade is, you can put it on the grinder and look up the resulting spark pattern; this will give you a good indication of its type. Of course you can also use it and see if it performs as you want it to, in which case it may not make any

difference what type it is. If you're buying or replacing a blade the following should give you some guidelines for your purchase.

CARBON STEEL

Carbon steel is the longstanding workhorse for manufacturing hand tools for woodworking. Carbon steel's qualities ideally meet the demands of hand tools for woodworking. With proper attention to its manufacture it can be brought to optimal sharpness for woodworking, will hold its edge, and can be re-sharpened easily—the three basic requirements of a woodworking blade. In addition, its manufacture can be varied slightly to accommodate different woodworking tasks. Many variations exist, based mostly on the quality of ingredients and manufacture, the composition of the original ore, how much it has been hot-worked, and what incidental alloys may be included. The quantity of alloys present may be more than incidental and not mentioned because the hand tool manufacturer has decided to present or allow the perception of its steel as carbon steel. Lumped into this general category are a number of types you will encounter commercially. Besides plain high-carbon steel, you will encounter (among others) *white steel, blue steel,* and *cast steel.*

While white and blue-steel are associated with Japanese tools, I mention them because they can be found in Japanese-made blades for Bailey planes. They derive their name from the color of the identifying paper label applied by the steel maker (usually Hitachi). Both have carbon in the 1% to 1.4% range with 0.1% to 0.2% silica and 0.2% to 0.3% manganese. *Blue paper steels* technically are alloy steels with 0.2% to 0.5% chromium and 1% to 1.5% tungsten, with up to 2.25% tungsten in the *super blue-steel*. The tungsten makes the blue-steel harder to forge but increases its wear resistance when cutting difficult woods. On the other hand, adding tungsten widens the critical temperature range needed for hardening the steel, and makes this step a little easier for the blacksmith. In contrast, some white-steels are fussy about their hardening temperatures. White steel is easier to sharpen, and takes the keen edge necessary for soft woods.

The difference between white and blue-steel is not immediately obvious. A Japanese woodworker I know makes an enlightened distinction between the two. He describes white-steel as having a sharp, angular grain structure, and blue-steel as having smaller, rounded grains. This allows the white-steel to be sharpened a nuance sharper, but under harsh conditions or with difficult woods white-steel's grain structure breaks off a little quicker and in slightly larger clumps. For that reason, dealers often recommend blue-steel for working hard, abrasive, or difficult tropical woods.

Cast steel, also called *crucible steel*, is brewed in small tightly controlled batches. The batches' small size and close monitoring are aimed at producing a high-quality steel of high predictability. It is an expensive process developed in Europe and America when producing quality steel was more of a craft than a manufacturing method. Over the years, as production methods improved, ever larger, cheaper, and more consistent batches of steel became possible. As the number of demanding craftsmen dropped, along with their market, particularly during the Great Depression, so, too, did the necessity for cast-steel. With World War II and a changing world economy, cast-steel all but disappeared and is now produced in only very small quantities.

Cast steel is a very fine-grained steel that, in my experience, takes and holds an edge that is far superior to most steels available today. Its qualities seem ideally suited to the demands of fine woodworking as it developed in the West prior to World War II, though it can be appreciated by demanding and discerning craftsmen today. With some few exceptions, I take the opportunity, when I can, to replace my modern blades with blades made of cast steel.

The edge steel of a cast-steel, white-steel, or blue-steel blade is too hard to use for the whole blade; it is too susceptible to shock and prone to cracking during use (it is also too expensive). Instead, a thin layer of it is forge-welded (laminated) to a back of softer

Figure 2-1. *A polished bevel on a cast-steel blade reveals the lamination of the two steels; the dark area across the edge of the blade at left is the edge steel, while the lighter area is the softer backing steel. At right is an unlaminated modern blade ground from bar stock. Bailey/ Stanley planes, at least into the 1930s (the date is arguable), had laminated blades, although the line is hard to discern on the bevel.*

steel that has more tensile strength. The combination is better able to absorb shock without breaking. Bailey planes, prior to World War II, had laminated blades. (See Figure 2-1.)

And then, of course, there is just "plain" carbon steel. Unless claims are made to the contrary this steel is usually cut from bar stock as it comes from the manufacturer with no additional hot work done to improve its structure. Plain carbon blades will probably offer disappointing performance. And while many premium after-market blades advertise having a higher degree of hardness than their competitors, unless the blades are forged, they will not have the improved grain structure that results from additional hot work.

So what are your options if (after reading the following section on alloy steels) you want to use a good quality, preferably forged, carbon steel blade? You do have some limited options. First, you can try and find a vintage laminated Stanley blade. These perform pretty well, though I'm not sure how easy they are to find. You also might be able to get

your hands on a Japanese-made blade that is laminated, though it appears you may have to order it from overseas. Lastly, if you want a 2" or 2⅜" blade you can order a hand-forged Clifton blade, which has given me good service.

ALLOY STEEL

Alloy steel was developed by and for industry, mostly in the early twentieth century, to cost-effectively produce large numbers of precisely engineered parts as might be used in cars—and nearly everything else we use now. I suspect the demands of World Wars I and II pushed development of alloys. While an alloy steel blade can be useful in some handplanes and woodworking hand tools, makers use cheaper mass-manufacturing processes mostly to imitate (with generally limited success) the quality blades previously achieved through skilled hot work of high-quality carbon steel.

Carbon steel has a number of shortcomings in industrial production. It hardens only to a depth of about ³⁄₁₆". Pieces of thick cross section do not harden all of the way through and their internal structure remains different from their surface structure. The differences compromise virtually any large machine application. In addition, the hardening process to produce this less-than-adequate structure requires quenching the red-hot steel in cold water. The shock of quenching usually distorts the object, and is, at least, unpredictable. If, after considerable time and effort milling a piece precisely to within a tolerance of several thousandths of an inch, the last step compromises the design tolerances, the product is rendered unusable. Lastly, when carbon steel is used for cutting tools to make other objects, especially out of metal or steel themselves, the speed of the cutter (or the object in relation to the cutter, as on a lathe) will overheat the blade, soften it, and cause it to lose its cutting ability within seconds.

Industry discovered adding small amounts of alloys eliminated many problems. The addition of chromium, for instance, allows steel of large cross-section to be hardened all the way through. Chromium and other alloys also produce steel that can be hardened in an oil bath, which is less shocking than water, and thus reduces dimensional distortion. Even better, some combinations of alloys allow the steel to harden in air, a slower, less-shocking process resulting in virtually no distortion. Many alloys produce steel that can be *red hard*; that is, even when heated by the friction of the cut to red hot, the steel will not lose its hardness, obviously very desirable in the manufacture of metal-cutting tools.

Eventually, a large number of recipes evolved to produce many different steels

ALLOY INGREDIENTS

Carbon added to iron makes it harder and more wear resistant. Carbon content of about 0.5% to 0.6% is about the lowest amount found in tool steel. The low carbon steel is used for hammers, blacksmith tools, etc. A carbon content of about 0.8% makes a steel file hard (about Rc 56–58). Carbon above that level does not increase the steel's hardness, but raises its wear resistance. A carbon content of 1.3% is about the highest. The highest-carbon steel is used for razors, engraving tools, etc. A carbon content of about 1.05% is a good average—hard with good wear resistance, and yet is not fussy or sensitive to heat.

Tungsten, added in small quantities, can impart a tight, small, and dense grain structure and the ability to attain a keen cutting edge. It also enables steel to retain its hardness at higher temperatures and has a detrimental effect on the steel's forgeability. A tungsten content of 4% (with 1.3% carbon) is so hard it is difficult to grind with an emery wheel.

Manganese makes steel sound when first cast into ingots, and easier to hot roll or forge. Practically all tool steel has at least 0.2% of manganese. Steel can contain up to 0.5% manganese before it is considered alloy steel.

Silicon facilitates casting and hot work. It usually is used in combination with manganese, molybdenum, or chromium. All steel has 0.1% to 0.3% silicon. Steel with 0.5% to 2% silicon content is considered an alloy.

Chromium increases the hardness penetration of the steel. A thick bar of plain carbon steel will be hardened to a depth of only 3/16" (5mm) from its face during heat treatment. Adding chromium allows the bar to harden all of the way through. Because most woodworking blades are less than 3/8" (10mm) thick, it is not really an issue for woodworkers. Chromium increases the steel's wear resistance under impact and heat, but does not necessarily increase its hardness. Steel with chromium content of 4% and higher is called *high-speed steel*.

for a variety of conditions. However, as the requirements of manufacturing metal parts for cars are different from those for woodworking hand tools, few alloy steels are useful to woodworkers. A small number are worth looking at if for no other reason than that they are regularly promoted to woodworkers.

The main difficulty when deciding whether to use alloyed steel is that adding alloys usually coarsens the grain and structure of the steel. Cutting wood cleanly and efficiently requires a fine blade edge. Coarsening the grain and structure of a hand tool blade reduces its effectiveness. Casual use of the few alloy steels used in hand tool blades may not show much difference between them and unalloyed blades. However, there is a difference, and it is more obvious in some woods and applications, which suggests the blades have special usefulness different from unalloyed carbon-steel blades.

Alloy steels are particularly suited for hard-use conditions. While they may not get as keen an edge as a finely wrought carbon-steel blade, their capacity for keeping their edge is excellent. As a result, they are a viable choice for spokeshaves, jack planes, and

FORGEABILTY

Because they remain hard while red hot, many alloy steels cannot be hot-worked (forged) or can be with great difficulty, and must be ground to shape. Many of the varieties, though, would not benefit from being forged.

carpentry chisels; where the stress of deep, repetitive cuts, grit, adhesives, and impact all take a toll on the edge. The steel, of course, does get sharp and may be a good choice for versatile tools such as the block plane, which may chamfer edges, remove glue, shape the edges of plywood, and smooth various surfaces, all on the same project.

Because alloyed steels cannot achieve the sharpness of carbon steel, I believe they are more suited to harder hardwoods, particularly tropicals, than to softwoods and softer hardwoods. Softwoods require a keen edge, though as the types of wood being worked increase in hardness and density, the importance of edge toughness increases. Tropical hardwoods require a demanding combination of keenness and toughness in equal proportions.

As to the third requirement for blades for woodworking hand tools, alloyed steels require different sharpening methods, increasingly so as the alloy content grows. The greater the alloy content, the less effective are waterstones and oilstones, necessitating a diamond stone or paste. The technique and the amount of time is about the same once the different abrasives are employed.

Some of the more common alloy steels woodworkers encounter are chrome vanadium, tungsten vanadium, PM-V11, occasionally D2 and M2, and more commonly O1 and A2. In the latter two, the *O* stands for *oil* hardening, the *A* for *air hardening*. O1 and A2 are two of only a few oil- and air-hardening steels that actually have an O or

A in their name. The numbers complete the name of that particular steel.

Chrome vanadium and tungsten vanadium are usually clearly marked on the blade and can be occasionally found on the blades of Bailey-style planes. These steels comprise a group of dozens of different recipes, of varying suitability (and quality). These blades are workhorses, not given to much subtlety, but often prove quite durable. They are well suited to heavy work. But while chrome vanadium and tungsten vanadium are suitable for many miscellaneous tasks

Figure 2-2. *Blades of alloyed steel are often marked, but not consistently so.*

around the shop (I think the target audience was the DIYer and the carpenter), both are coarser grained and it is difficult to make fine, tearout-free shavings in many woods. (See Figure 2-2.)

PM-V11 is one of a group of new steels made using powdered metal technology. The PM stands for powdered metal and I assume the V11 stands for 11% vanadium, which is quite high. The technology results in a steel of very consistent grain size. This along with its high alloy content has, according to testing and many reviews, resulted in a steel that outlasts virtually all the other steels commonly used for plane blades, and is, in addition, easy to sharpen. It would seem to be an ideal all-around blade steel. The jury is out, though, on just how sharp you can get it, though it would seem for most uses—sharp enough.

D2 and M2 show up now and then, though often identified only as high-speed steel. Both of these are very high in chromium (11% to 13% and 3.75% to 4.5%, respectively) with M2 having over 6% tungsten as well. They exhibit classic alloy steel characteristics: extremely durable edge, but they don't get very sharp and they are very difficult to sharpen. For most uses these steels are not suitable for plane blades.

A2 steel blades have gained prominence as the apparent answer to both the manufacturers' desire for affordable quality and consistency and the woodworker's interest in satisfactory performance. A2 steel is more finely grained than chrome vanadium and tungsten vanadium blades,

but rivals their durability. Additionally, higher-end blades are cryogenically treated. In theory, the cryogenic process hardens the blade similar to heat-treating by causing the growth of carbides (crystals that cause steel to harden) but without enlarging the crystal structure, as can happen during heat treatment. Actual evidence this is happening is inconclusive, and anecdotal evidence from woodworkers suggests it is difficult to tell any difference between cryogenically treated and untreated blades. Regardless of whether they are cryogenically treated or not, the sharpenability of the blades varies by manufacturer. I have one blade I sharpen on waterstones while another requires diamond stones. You will have to discover what works best for your blades. (See Figure 2-3.)

A2 blades promise performance across a spectrum of tasks and difficult woods, and may become the new industry standard (though we'll have to wait and see if it's supplanted by the new PM-V11). Aiming toward a least common denominator, however, compromises performance at both ends of the spectrum. Fine smoothing in softwoods and many hardwoods is not as effective with an A2 blade because it does not take a thin bevel well (25° or less), and a blade with higher alloy content better handles heavy work in tropical hardwoods.

O1 tool steel is another alloy blade now available. O1 has one-tenth the chromium

Figure 2-3. *Blades of A2 steel are usually marked. The one at left was cryogenically treated and is labeled as such.*

of A2. It's a generally finer grain steel than A2 without the coarseness resulting from the addition of so much chromium. Its lower chromium content makes it easier to sharpen and it should (depending on quality) take a keener edge than A2. Additionally, because it has some tungsten and vanadium in it, it should show greater endurance in shaping tasks than carbon steel.

MY RECOMMENDATION

Unless you are dissatisfied with the performance of the blade you currently have in your plane I wouldn't change it. If after you've used the plane for a while, you find the longevity of the edge disappointing for the use you're giving it, or you are unable to get tearout-free results with a well set-up plane, I would consider replacing the blade as follows: planes used for heavy stock removal, a good tungsten- or chrome-vanadium blade or a PM-V11 blade (I have not been impressed with A2 for stock removal). For general purpose work probably a PM-V11 blade (I say this with the reservation that I haven't used this steel) or an A2 blade. For fine smoothing of softwoods and hardwoods probably O1 or a cast-steel blade, with A2 and then PM-V11 being used as the wood gets harder and the blade angle higher.

HIGH-SPEED STEEL

Further out yet on the scale of alloy steels is high-speed steel (HSS), which has chromium, vanadium, tungsten, and others (but mainly chromium) added in relatively high percentages. HSS is essentially the same steel used in drill and other power-driven bits, and is very hard and tough. Industry originally developed HSS to work at red-hot temperatures while remaining hard enough to maintain its cutting edge. For the woodworker, there are two main problems with the use of HSS, the same problems associated with the alloy steels, only multiplied several times over. The first is the difficulty in sharpening. While alloy steels are difficult to hone on the more common sharpening stone, HSS is impossible. Some steels are even difficult to grind. A diamond stone or diamond paste is a necessity, which is probably more a nuisance than a problem. The second problem with HSS is it does not get as sharp as carbon steel or even alloy steel. The grain of HSS is coarser than alloy

steel—so it has limitations.

Its only possible use in plane blades would be in very high blade-angle planes (60° and above) used on tropical hardwoods. Here the edge could be sharp enough for this near scraping cut and the durability would be a definite asset. I have seen modern Chinese-style planes use HSS blades and the blades in other traditional Chinese planes also appear to have high alloy content. Coupled with the heat generated by the hardness and abrasive quality of the woods, HSS could make sense here.

The option to choose a blade of one type of steel or another is one of the great advantages woodworkers have today. Understanding the qualities of each in the face of contradictory claims and explanations allows us to choose one over another and expedite the work. Knowledge and practice allows us to match the blade to the tool and the tool to the work.

3

TACTICS FOR ACHIEVING BEST PERFORMANCE

Understanding How a Plane Works

Chapter 3 discusses in detail the anatomical features common to all handplanes—and the tactics for optimal quality and efficiency they make possible—both individually and in their interaction with one another. Later chapters demonstrate how techniques traditionally were employed in various combinations to dimension, join, and smooth lumber by using the jack, jointer, and smoothing planes; their use in other types of planes; and how a modern user can put his or her own combination of techniques together to achieve fast and effective results.

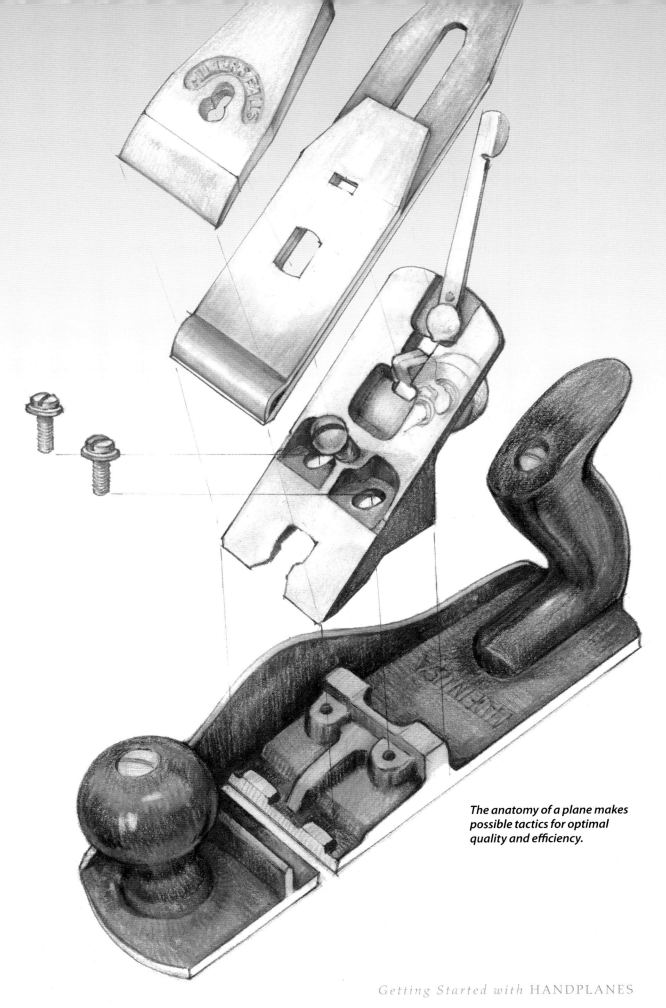

The anatomy of a plane makes
possible tactics for optimal
quality and efficiency.

HOW TO USE THIS CHAPTER

The information throughout this book should serve beginner and experienced woodworkers alike. For some beginners, however, this chapter might be too much information. Glance over it and absorb what you can. If it seems too much, rather than risk frustration, it may be better set up your plane as best you can, following the basic guidelines set out in the following chapter on bench planes, and begin work. After you have used your plane for a while, Chapter 3 will make more sense, and you will be better able to apply its advice. You will have to read Chapter 3 eventually, because the information here is fundamental to setting up, tuning, modifying, and troubleshooting your plane.

THE TACTICS

The core tactics for efficient, effective performance involve six common anatomical features:

1. **Angle of the blade to the work.** Using planes with blade angles suited to the wood or to the task increases a plane's reliability and efficiency.

2. **Clearance of the mouth through which the shaving passes.** Little understood and often abused, a suitable mouth opening controls, if not eliminates, tearout.

3. **The use of a chipbreaker.** A relatively recent invention that nearly eliminates tearout while increasing a plane's versatility.

4. **Angle of the blade's bevel.** Not having the correct blade bevel angle causes many headaches.

5. **Shape of the blade edge.** The re-sharpened edges of a plane's blade are not all straight— in fact, few of them are.

6. **Length of the plane body and width of the blade.** The two have a relationship to each other and define a plane's intended use.

The Angle of the Blade

To be more accurate, the *angle of the blade* (Figure 3-1) should be called the angle of the cutting edge. It is the angle at which the cutting edge is presented to the work. On

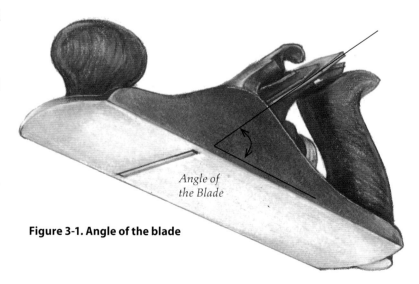

Angle of the Blade

Figure 3-1. Angle of the blade

blades with the bevel down toward the work, it is the angle of the blade as positioned in the plane, sometimes called the bedding angle. On blades with the bevel up, it is the bedding angle plus the angle of the bevel (Figure 3-2).

While the bevel-down Stanley/Bailey plane only ever came with a 45° bedding angle, this angle doesn't work well for everything. It is perhaps the most versatile angle, working pretty well for softwoods and most hardwoods (though not too well on tropical hardwoods), but will cause extra work in some woods and for doing some tasks. If you find yourself working in these woods or doing these tasks, there are a few things you can do to get a more efficient blade angle. This will be discussed in detail as we go along.

TRADITIONAL BLADE ANGLES

Looking at traditional tools, the precursors of the Stanley/Bailey-style handplanes now commonly available, you can see that using planes with different blade angles (or *pitch*, as it is called in Britain) was a common practice. Variations in blade angles among traditional tools are large and obvious, within the tradition of a particular culture and from culture to culture. The difference in blade angles between a classic Chinese furniture plane and a traditional Japanese carpenter's plane, for instance, is striking.

I believe such differences exist because individual woodworking trades within each culture tended to work on a limited number of typically indigenous woods. Over time, woodworkers discovered certain cutting angles worked better on these woods, so blade angles on the tools within these trades usually occupied a narrow range. Additionally, you see similarities in the blade angles of tools within the same trades right across different cultures, as they often used similar species of wood. Finally, historically,

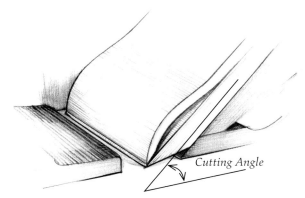

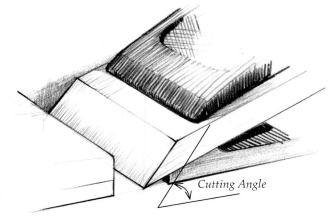

Figure 3-2. *The cutting angle is the angle that the cutting edge presents to the work. On blades with the bevel down (above), it is the angle of the blade in the plane (the bedding angle). On blades with the bevel up (right), it is the angle of the blade in the plane plus the angle of the bevel.*

Figure 3-3. *A set of Chinese cabinet-makers' planes, back to front: jointer with a 55° pitch; intermediate smoother with a 60° pitch; smoother with a 65° pitch. The high pitches of the blades are for working tropical hardwoods. (The hole through the body is for a crosshandle, which has been removed for the photo.)*

PITCH ANGLES

While Western blade angles are usually measured in degrees, the pitch of a Japanese plane blade is determined using a rise/run scale based on 10 rather than degrees. That is why you will sometimes come across such apparently odd pitches as 47½°, which is actually a rise of 11 in a run of 10. Curiously, these pitches can be found also in English planes. Norris planes often had a pitch of 47½°, and I have an American razee try plane with a 43° blade angle (a 9 in 10 pitch). As it turns out, these are my favorite blade angles for smoothing wood; 43° does a nice job on many of the softer hardwoods as well as maple, and 47½° works well on many of the harder hardwoods. The latter pitch also seems to be a critical angle around which the geometry of the cut begins to change.

you can see the changes the introduction of new woods through international trade brought to the tools.

This effect on plane anatomy attributable to the material being worked is most striking in the planes of Chinese and Southeast Asian furniture makers (Figure 3-3). Traditional furniture in these cultures is typically made of rosewood or some similar tropical hardwood. The cutting angle of these planes is very high. Truing planes, usually the first to be used and making the heaviest cut, have cutting angles around 55°. Intermediate smoothing planes have angles around 60°. The cutting angle of the final plane is often over 65°.

Northern Europeans, working with indigenous hardwoods such as oak, birch, and walnut, and using deal (pine or fir) and other species as secondary woods, have planes with cutting angles ranging from about 40° for preliminary to about 55° for finish planes, with 60° and 64° often used for molding planes (Figure 3-4, Figure 3-5).

The carpentry tradition of Japan is exquisitely refined and sophisticated, and most of the tools imported from there reflect it. The woods worked are largely softwoods such as cedar, with elm and some similar woods also encountered. The majority of planes commonly imported have an angle of 40°, though in response to the American market, planes with higher blade angles are now occasionally brought in.

Figure 3-4. *In this set of traditional wood planes, the higher the pitch, the smoother the surface produced. From back to front: try plane with a 43° pitch; jointer with a 47½° pitch; smoother with a 50° pitch.*

THE BEST BLADE ANGLE

The inference of all this, and a fact borne out in practice, is that softer woods take a lower cutting angle than the harder woods. Conversely, the harder the wood, the higher the angle. This is not always true, but it is a good starting point. I would add: Use the lowest cutting angle that remains effective, for two reasons. The lower angle shears wood fibers rather than scrapes them, producing a better surface. The lower angle also involves less work as the shearing cut presents less resistance than the scraping cut.

A couple of factors interplay with this rule of thumb. First, softwoods, hardwoods, and tropical hardwoods each respond differently to the cutting action of the blade. Second, end grain cuts differently than long grain.

Softwoods require cutting, not scraping. The higher cutting angles that, in hardwoods, produce successful compression failure (Type-II chips, per Bruce Hoadly in Understanding Wood) will only tear the fibers in softwoods, causing the chip to crumple into a bunch

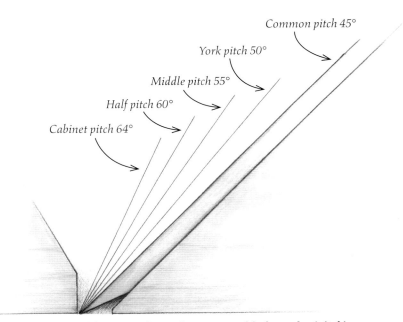

Figure 3-5. British nomenclature for common blade angles (pitch).

Common pitch 45°
York pitch 50°
Middle pitch 55°
Half pitch 60°
Cabinet pitch 64°

WHY 45°?

Because the majority of woodworkers work in hardwoods, the question arises—why do manufacturers use a softwood angle for their planes? I think the answer lies in the evolution of the tool. The Bailey-type plane is a general-use plane, for carpentry as well as cabinetwork, meant to perform a variety of tasks—a least common denominator that appeals to the widest market. The 45° blade angle allows use of the plane for the widest variety of woods. The 45° angle is low enough that it will cut softwoods but is not so low it cannot deal with many of the more common hardwoods. It is a compromise angle—it cuts well in a few woods, and is serviceable with all the rest.

CUTTING ANGLES FOR DIFFERENT WOODS

As a general rule of thumb, the cutting angle for softwoods varies from 35° to around 45° with the lower end working best. Cutting angles for hardwoods run the gamut from about 40° to 55° and higher, though the majority work well in the 45° to 50° range. Tropical hardwood cutting angles range from about 50° to over 65°.

CUTTING END GRAIN

End grain is best cut at the lowest possible angle: in practice about 22°—or about the size of the bevel of a paring chisel—which works quite well for shearing end grain, but is hard to control. The traditional solution, rather than use a blade one face of which would be flush to the work as a paring chisel would be, was to mount a blade in a plane at a low angle (12° to 18°) with the bevel up. The arrangement, somewhat compromising of performance on end grain, gains the advantages of control, adjustability, jigging (provided by the sole of the plane), and the ability to plane end grain with some reliability.

A number of planes are set up like this, the most familiar being the Stanley 60½, which can be used on a shooting board to plane board ends, as well as perform the multitude of other tasks it is often called upon to do. Another plane of note was the Stanley 62 low-angle jack plane (now remade by Lie-Nielsen, Veritas, and others). Shoulder planes, a joint-making plane discussed in Chapter 6, developed mainly from a need to even out the end grain of poorly cut tenon shoulders.

USE THE LOWEST EFFECTIVE CUTTING ANGLE

The lower the angle the cleaner the shear. The higher the angle (increasingly above 47½°) the more it cuts like a scraper. At an angle around 75° or 80°, the tool is best regarded as a scraper.

(Figure 3-6). A scraper will shape, but not actually smooth, softwood.

Hardwoods are somewhat on the cusp between softwoods and tropical hardwoods. Hardwoods often respond well to a sharp low-angle blade, but can also be smoothed, more or less, with just a scraper. The wide variety of grain structures and hardness within this group suggests a variety of cutting angles can be used. For this reason low-to-medium blade angles work well, though higher blade angles are sometimes safer and more predictable, producing less tearout with less adjustment, maintenance, and sharpening. The resulting surface, though, is not as smooth or clear as with a lower-angle cut.

Tropical hardwoods respond well to scraping, conversely tearing out disastrously at low and intermediate blade angles. Traditional blade angles for tropicals often are quite high—at what would be a scraping angle in a softer wood. Despite the high angle, the plane blade leaves a clean-cut surface with good clarity.

There is a great deal of overlap where angles work well in a particular wood. Often the same angle seems less effective from one

Figure 3-6. Blade angles for different woods
Within the range for each wood the lower angles are generally for preparatory planes; the higher angles are for smoothing planes.

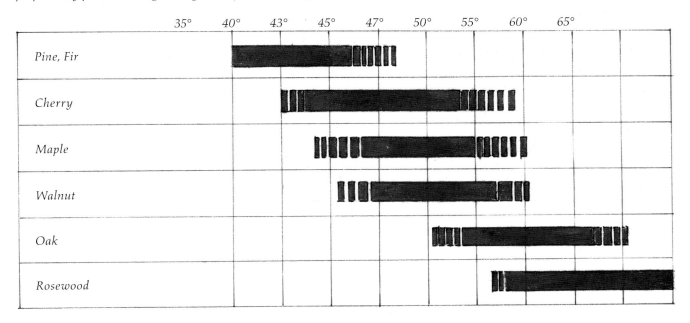

board to another in the same species, or even from one part of a board to another. Because of such variations, most woodworkers use more conservative angles—slightly steeper but within the acceptable range—for more predictable results and little or no tearout.

Finally, you will find some blade angles cannot be used when planing some woods. It is not that they do not plane well, but that they nearly do not plane at all. Pine, for instance, seems to crumple as the blade angle increases over 45°. Results can be disastrous with some tropical hardwoods at even the intermediate blade angles.

BLADE ANGLE AND THE TASK

Studying traditional tools also shows the cutting angle of a plane blade depends upon the task being performed. Because a lower-angle blade presents less resistance

BLADE STEELS FOR DIFFERENT WOODS

Softwoods respond best to a fine-grained steel blade sharpened to a thin, sharp edge, mounted at a low angle for a shearing cut. For this reason, a high-quality hand-forged carbon-steel blade is the best choice for smoothing softwood.

Though the sharpness of a fine-grained edge is not as critical, North American and European hardwoods respond best to a sharp edge. For final tearout-free smoothing, a finely wrought carbon-steel blade remains the best choice, though a fine grain alloy steel often yields satisfactory results.

Tropical hardwoods are less sensitive to the thinness of the cutting edge. Tropical hardwoods do not demand the sharpness required by the softwoods and most hardwoods for good results. They cut best with a high-angle blade—more of a scraping cut. The wood's hardness generates a fair amount of heat at the blade's edge. Under such conditions, and considering the abrasive nature of some of these woods, a thin edge is more susceptible to rapid dulling, minor chipping, or other damage. Using a good fine-grained alloy steel blade makes sense here.

MOLDING PLANES

The practice of using higher blade angles on molding versus smoothing planes for hardwoods suggests two things:
- increasing the blade's angle increases the *reliability* of the cut;
- increasing the blade's pitch above the normal range reduces cut *quality*.

Increasing the blade angle is the default for reducing tearout on a molding plane.

Many molding planes use pitches in excess of the normal range—often as high as 64°—that would be found in planes used on the same wood. Experience with molding planes confirms that while this might produce a surface with minor roughness, it largely avoids more disastrous forms of tearout. A reduced-quality cut was the better choice for the eighteenth-century craftsman who used these tools, than a higher quality cut punctuated with deep tearout.

The goal of smoothing work for the eighteenth-century craftsman was to achieve an acceptable surface straight from the plane or scraper, and to absolutely minimize the use of glasspaper. Glasspaper, the precursor to sandpaper, was usually made by the craftsman himself, by pulverizing an expensive piece of glass, and sieving and sifting it onto paper coated with hide glue. It worked slowly, wore out quickly, and was effective only for polishing—not removing anything more than minor imperfections. The craftsman aimed for a surface from his molding plane that required only minor, if any, glass papering. Moldings produced by high pitch molding planes would be acceptable.

in cutting than a higher-angle blade with its scraping cut, planes used for shaping or preparing stock tend to have lower angles. Lower-cutting angles are less fatiguing because the plane requires less effort to push. At this stage in the work, stock removal is more important than smoothness, which can be accomplished with succeeding planes. Traditionally, craftsmen use several planes to take a board from initial surfacing to final smoothing. Each succeeding plane had a slightly steeper pitch, usually finishing with

a plane the craftsman determines has the optimal angle for the work produced.

CUSTOM BLADE ANGLES

One way is to alter the angle of the bevel on the blade itself, which is easiest in planes with the bevel of the blade mounted up such as the Stanley 60½ or any of the new bevel-up planes made by Lie-Nielsen or Veritas. Because the bevel is mounted up, any change in its angle changes the cutting angle. The disadvantage is that increasing the bevel angle often results in an angle blunter than normally desirable, cutting action is reduced, the surface is not cut as cleanly, the edge may dull quicker (it was blunter to begin with), and the plane requires greater effort to push. (See "Bevel Angle" on page 50.)

In planes with the bevel mounted down, you can back-bevel a blade. This is where you put a second bevel on the topside of the blade, opposite to the main bevel. This is usually a small bevel established by honing rather than by grinding. I would do this only for the occasional piece. If you find yourself working repeatedly with woods that require a different angle, it will be more efficient to buy or make a plane to that angle, or at least buy a second blade and chipbreaker, so you don't have to regrind the blade every time you change.

When you work much with a plane, you sharpen frequently, sometimes every 15 to 20 minutes, depending on the fineness of the work. Repeating a finely angled back-bevel can become a nuisance. In addition, back beveling may require the main bevel to be reground as the bevel becomes larger and more blunt, which reduces the blade's cutting action. When you finally remove the back-bevel, you have to grind that much of the blade away to restore the original edge. On the other hand, back beveling can be an efficient solution for less frequent plane users or for those occasional situations that really do not warrant the time required to make or set up a plane specifically for that task. (If you are interested in exploring this topic further, check out *Double Bevel Sharpening* by Brian Burns.)

Skewing the plane in use is another way to vary the blade angle. Craftsmen who plane a lot do it instinctively in response to the feedback from the wood. They may do it over the whole board or only those sections of it that respond better to the technique. Skewing the plane effectively lowers the blade angle, and presents a thinner bevel to the wood (Figure 3-7).

It works sometimes for these reasons, but I think it is usually successful more because you are approaching a section of difficult grain from a more successful direction, which may be different from the general direction of the grain of the board. I usually skew the plane only to change the angle of attack. Keeping the blade sharp usually works better. Nor would I use this tactic as a substitute for a plane built with the correct blade angle.

Recently, Lee Valley has introduced their series of customizable planes. These include, among other things, the ability to customize blade angles by ordering frogs (the blade's bed) in different angles. This is a marvelous solution, but it is expensive. However, I'm assuming the frogs are interchangeable, allowing the use of a single plane body to have different blade angles, and thereby at least eliminating the need to have a separate plane for each blade angle.

A surprising amount of tearout at any angle is avoidable by having an extremely sharp blade (this is borne out in tests conducted and photographed recently in Japan). Here is where you start to notice the difference between what is just sharp, and what is extremely sharp. Your first clue comes in the midst of working: your plane, a finely set smoother, while still cutting effectively now occasionally leaves some tearout. You stop and sharpen it and now

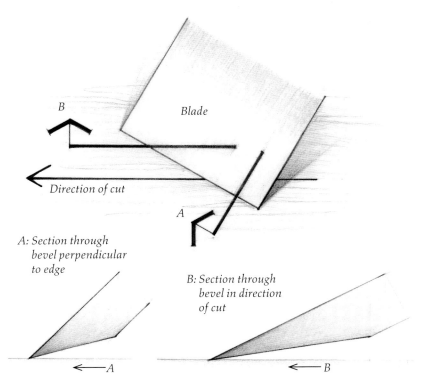

Figure 3-7. *If the blade is skewed when planing, the effective bevel angle (as presented to the wood) is smaller than the actual ground bevel.*

those problem areas of tearout can be cut cleanly again. The only thing you changed is the blade sharpness. It makes a difference. I have lower-angle blades that often work better than higher-angle blades in a wood I know prefers a higher cutting angle, only because the quality of the blade is better—it just gets and stays sharper.

Mouth Opening

Controlling the shaving as it passes through the opening in the bottom of the plane is probably the second-most basic technique for controlling tearout, but one that is not well understood (Figure 3-8). Restricting the mouth opening works to reduce tearout (Figure 3-9) by compressing the wood fibers immediately in front of the blade, thus keeping them from splitting out ahead of the cut (Figure 3-10). While it is an effective tactic, it has become a less popular one for a number of reasons.

For one, the amount of openness is a dynamic factor, affected by the combination of blade angle, chipbreaker bevel angle, and escape angle of the throat (Figure 3-11).

Figure 3-8. Mouth opening.

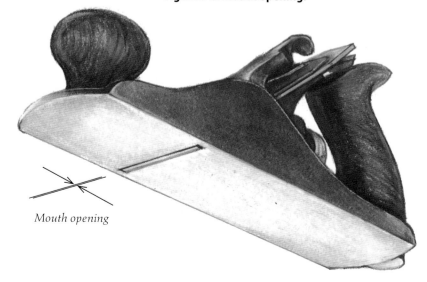

Mouth opening

The result of such complexity is easy to misjudge, and can be frustrating. If the mouth is too small for the cut, the shavings jam in the throat, which can damage the edge of the mouth and sometimes the blade. Restricting the chip at the mouth of the plane definitely increases stress on the blade, as both pressure and heat build. The increased downward pressure on the blade due to the chip being constricted as it passes through the mouth—made even greater at the higher blade angles—increases the importance of the correct bevel angle, as the blade edge is liable to flex (see "Bevel Angle" on page 50). When this happens, it flexes deeper into the cut, taking a slightly thicker chip (Figure 3-12). The result is one of three things: tearout, a chattering cut (as the blade flexes back and forth), or a chip too large for the opening, which causes the chip to jam.

Closing the mouth down also increases the wear on the edge of the mouth itself. For maximum effectiveness, the edge of the mouth should be crisp. Sharp is even better. The increased pressure from constricting the chip eventually rounds the edge over, and the rounder it gets, the less effective it is.

Increased heat build-up at the mouth is palpable. The oils in the wood being planed vaporize and condense on the top edge of the blade, causing a superficial discoloration of the blade just above the edge. Sometimes when you disassemble a blade and chipbreaker to sharpen it you will see evidence of this discoloration on both of them.

Though work hardening of a plane blade seems like a woodworking myth, when you see evidence of this kind of heat, you begin to think that perhaps some change in the steel might be occurring. Increased heat build-up does speed deterioration of the edge. Use of an alloy blade in a high-angle plane can slow this deterioration.

The interrelationship of the mouth opening to the other anatomical tactics is dynamic. The effectiveness of restricting the mouth opening varies according to the blade angle. While effective at lower angles, it seems more so at higher blade angles (50°+) and practice confirms it. The chipbreaker, however, seems to be less effective on higher-angle planes and increasingly effective as blade angle drops below 50°. On planes with angles greater than 50°, I often rely on a small mouth opening alone to control tearout.

Without an adjustable mouth, finish planing is the only task you can do with a plane so configured because the mouth is too narrow for other work. You will need more planes because a single tool will not do a variety of tasks as designed. This is not necessarily a bad thing as I believe you will find the set-up and maintenance of a fine finish plane does not lend itself to the plane doing less-refined tasks, mouth opening or not, intended versatility or not. Fine-finish planing is demanding, and having dedicated planes set up for it is a timesaver.

Figure 3-9. *Unrestrained shaving splits out ahead of cut, causing tearout.*

Figure 3-10. *Shaving restrained by a tight mouth opening prevents shaving from lifting ahead of the cut, reducing or eliminating tearout.*

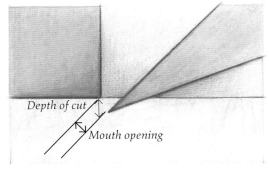

Depth of cut

Mouth opening

Figure 3-11. *For maximum effectiveness against tearout, the mouth opening is equal to the depth of cut. In the real world, the mouth may have to be ever so slightly larger, but definitely no less than the depth of cut.*

Figure 3-12. *A mouth opening or a bevel angle that is too small can cause the edge to flex.*

ADJUSTING THE MOUTH OPENING

Most metal planes today have a way of adjusting the mouth opening. Two ways have been developed to do this. The first (and least effective, I believe) is the frog adjustment found on traditional Bailey bevel-down planes. The concept is that the frog, or moveable bed of the blade, adjusts forward (along with the blade), thus reducing the mouth opening. The adjustment is cumbersome, takes time, and when moved forward the blade cantilevers off the frog leaving it susceptible to chatter. On the Bedrock models, the frog slides down and forward, supporting the blade closer to the edge. With this configuration, a precise mouth opening still requires some fiddling back and forth with both the blade and frog adjustments. This is discussed in greater detail in Chapter 4.

The best method for adjusting the mouth is the sliding mouthpiece, set into the sole of the plane in front of the blade. Most commonly found on metal block planes and other low-angle metal planes, and now on a few new bevel-down planes, this is a very effective, quick, and easy method for adjusting the throat while the blade remains firmly bedded.

Chipbreaker

The chipbreaker (Figure 3-13) is a 300- to 400-year-old invention that has increased the reliability of the handplane in getting consistently smooth results. The chipbreaker accomplishes this through one main

mechanism and some secondary ones. The primary mechanism for improving consistency of the cut gives the piece its name: By sharpening the bevel on the chipbreaker and placing it directly behind the cutting edge (Figure 3-14), the chip is broken backward before it has a chance to lift and split ahead of the cut (Figure 3-15). This has proven to be a highly effective method

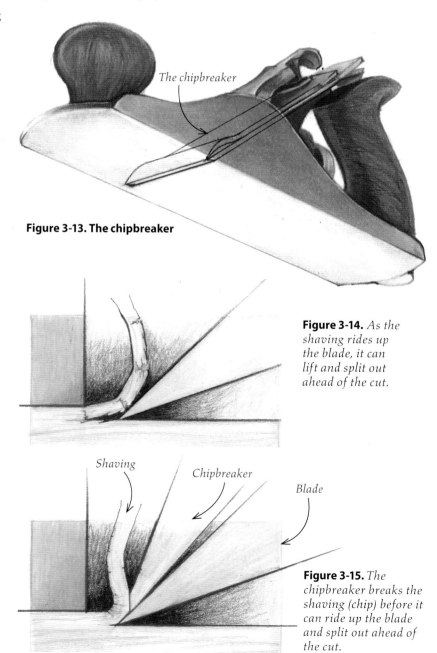

The chipbreaker

Figure 3-13. The chipbreaker

Figure 3-14. *As the shaving rides up the blade, it can lift and split out ahead of the cut.*

Shaving

Chipbreaker

Blade

Figure 3-15. *The chipbreaker breaks the shaving (chip) before it can ride up the blade and split out ahead of the cut.*

PLANE GEOMETRY, A SUMMARY

The interrelationship between blade angle, mouth opening, chipbreaker, throat angle, and bevel angle is dynamic **(Figure 1)**. When constructing or tuning a plane, keep the interplay in mind and adjust each element according to the other. Some *single-bladed planes*, of course, do not have a chipbreaker. Planes with a chipbreaker are sometimes called *double-iron planes*.

Figure 1. Definitions

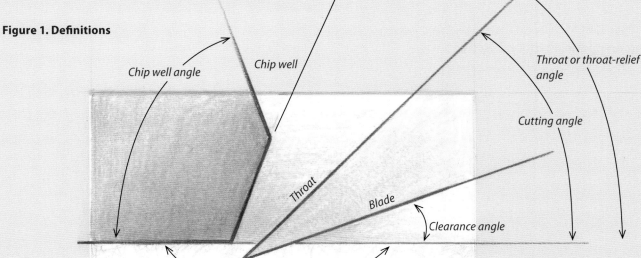

Chip well angle

Chip well

Throat or throat-relief angle

Cutting angle

Throat

Blade

Clearance angle

Sole

BEVEL-UP PLANES

On bevel-up planes and other planes without a chipbreaker, the mouth opening should be the same size or perhaps slightly larger than the thickest shaving you intend to make with that plane. For roughing out and dimensioning, the opening could be 1/32" to 1/16" (0.8mm to 2mm) or greater **(Figure 2)**. On intermediate smoothing planes, a mouth opening of 0.01" (0.25mm) or less is useful **(Figure 3)**. For your finest finishing cuts, the mouth opening could be just several thousandths of an inch or about the size of a fine shaving—usually just open enough you can see light through it when you look in from the top **(Figure 4)**.

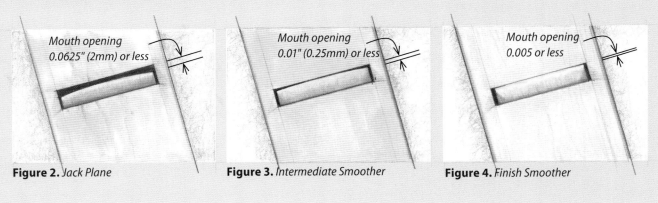

Mouth opening 0.0625" (2mm) or less

Figure 2. *Jack Plane*

Mouth opening 0.01" (0.25mm) or less

Figure 3. *Intermediate Smoother*

Mouth opening 0.005 or less

Figure 4. *Finish Smoother*

BEVEL-UP PLANES *continued*

The angle of the throat opening need be only 15°
to 20° greater than the cutting angle, but usually
not less than 70° **(Figure 5)**.

You want to keep the throat angle as small
as possible because as the plane wears and the
bottom is trued repeatedly, the mouth opens
(Figure 6). Keeping the angle as small as possible
slows this process. If your plane has a moveable
mouth plate, you avoid the problem.

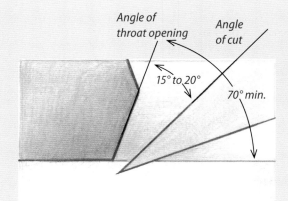

Figure 5. *Relationship of
the Throat Angle to the
Cutting Angle*

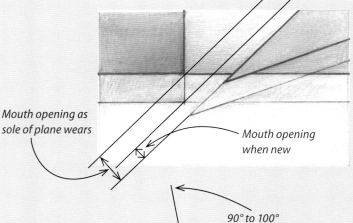

Figure 6. *As the sole of
the plane wears and is
flattened repeatedly, the
mouth opening gradually
increases in size.*

BEVEL DOWN PLANES

Sharpen the working edge on a chipbreaker so it is
90° to 100° to the sole when mounted in the plane.
Use the higher angle on low-blade-angle planes,
the lower angle on high-blade-angle planes
(Figure 7).

For maximum reduction of tearout, the
chipbreaker should be set back from the edge
a distance equal to about the thickness of the
shaving to be cut. Depending on the curvature,
the setback often equals the sweep of the blade.
Of course, the chipbreaker should not be set below
the bottom of the plane **(Figure 8)**.

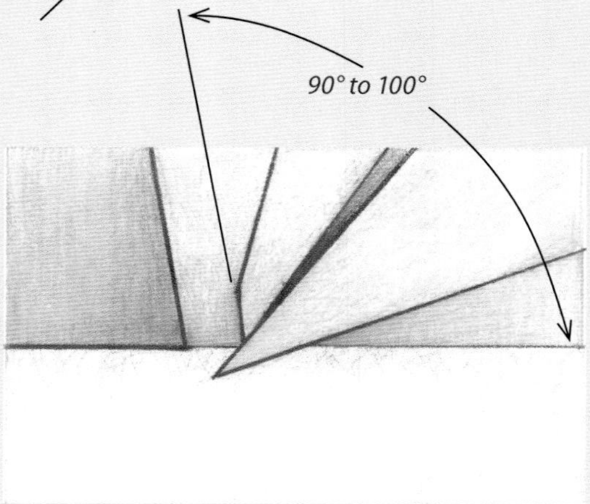

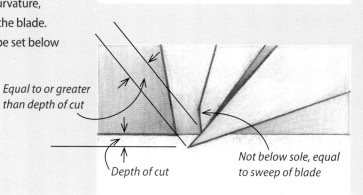

Figure 7. *Angle of the
Working Bevel of the
Chipbreaker*

Figure 8. *Chipbreaker
Setback*

At all points, the opening for the shaving to pass must be greater than the thickness of the shaving itself. If you are trying to maximize the effect of a small mouth opening in combination with the use of a chipbreaker, the throat angle would have to be equal to, or preferably greater than, the combined angle of the blade and chipbreaker bevel, or between 90° and 100°—maybe slightly more (**Figure 9**).

Any more, however, and the edge of the mouth can become too thin, wearing extremely quickly and sometimes even flexing under the pressure of the constrained shaving, causing the shaving to jam the throat. As the bottom of the plane flattens, the mouth also wears open quickly.

A plane set up with the smallest mouth opening and tightest chipbreaker setting can make only the finest, thinnest of cuts. For smoothing planes requiring more versatility, especially in the low-to-intermediate blade angles, it is more practical to rely mostly on the chipbreaker to eliminate tearout, with the mouth opening in a supporting role (**Figure 10**). Such a strategy allows a reduced throat angle that will slow the gradual enlargement of the mouth opening as the sole is conditioned. In this case, the mouth opening would be no more than 1/64" (0.4mm). Clearance for the shaving through the throat must be maintained, however.

Because the throat angle is not parallel to the working edge of the chipbreaker in this setup, the high point of the chipbreaker is where the shaving tends to jam. In this case, it is helpful to have the edge of the chipbreaker ground with a second, main bevel of about 25°, with the working edge shaped to a microbevel of about 1/32" (0.8mm), rather than the more rounded profile seen on many chipbreakers. This may not be possible with the Bailey-type chipbreaker. In preparing the chipbreaker, be certain it was not rounded over more than its original shape. It is easy to stroke the top of the chipbreaker when preparing the edge

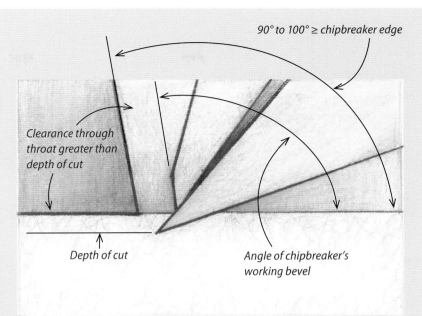

90° to 100° ≥ chipbreaker edge

Clearance through throat greater than depth of cut

Depth of cut

Angle of chipbreaker's working bevel

Figure 9. *The angle of the chipbreaker's working bevel.*

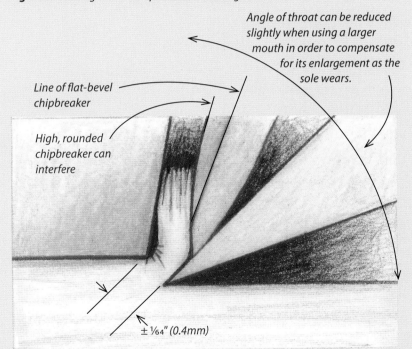

Angle of throat can be reduced slightly when using a larger mouth in order to compensate for its enlargement as the sole wears.

Line of flat-bevel chipbreaker

High, rounded chipbreaker can interfere

± 1/64" (0.4mm)

Figure 10. *To increase a plane's versatility, especially in planes with a blade angle of 47½° or less, it's more practical to rely on the chipbreaker than the mouth opening to reduce tearout. On a smoothing plane, however, you'll still want a mouth opening of about 1/64" (0.4mm).*

with an overextended rotating motion that increases the curve, steepens the angle, and constricts the chip.

of reducing tearout, especially when coupled with a small mouth opening at lower-to-medium blade angles.

There are at least three distinct shapes of chipbreaker. One (typical on modern premium Bailey planes, older, wooden planes, and Japanese planes) consists of a large flat bevel ground at about 25° (measured when mounted to the blade), with a secondary, smaller bevel that does the work (Figure 3-16).

A second shape, seen on both new and old manufactured wood planes, is similar in profile, only slightly rounded rather than beveled (Figure 3-17).

The third shape, most often seen on the Stanley/Bailey planes, is a bulbous, almost semicircular curve near the blade edge (Figure 3-18).

On most planes, the Bailey style included, the first shape is probably the most versatile, because the large, low bevel provides more clearance for the shaving broken by the smaller bevel. Rounded chipbreakers constrict the throat more, resulting in a greater chance the shavings will jam. (See "Plane Geometry, A Summary" on page 43.)

The second type, slightly rounded, will usually work satisfactorily, and is used on Clifton's Sta-Set chipbreaker (see next page), but if you have problems with jamming, consider filing the rounded shape to a flat secondary bevel (assuming you are left with enough material not to weaken the

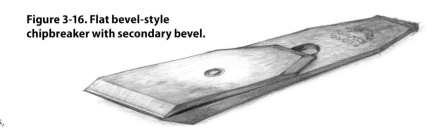

Figure 3-16. Flat bevel-style chipbreaker with secondary bevel.

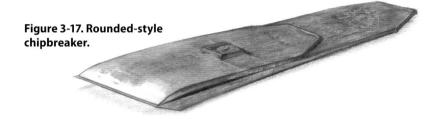

Figure 3-17. Rounded-style chipbreaker.

Figure 3-18. Stanley-type chipbreaker.

HARD CHIPBREAKERS

Good quality Japanese planes have chipbreakers and main blades laminated with a hard steel edge. Sometimes on the lesser-quality Japanese planes, the chipbreaker is tempered, not laminated. You might think this is excessive, but it is not. Using a chipbreaker in a position tight to the cutting edge subjects it to a lot of impact and heat. It will dull and needs to be resharpened over time, and if it is not, it may begin to trap chips. I have seen soft chipbreakers get a multitude of tiny dents from just the impact of the shaving. I also have seen the discoloration on the edge from the oils in the wood vaporizing with the heat of the cut. Having a hard chipbreaker reduces maintenance and improves reliability.

chipbreaker itself). I would try this fix before opening the throat angle.

The third type, generally seen only on Bailey planes, with its bulbous rounding (perhaps meant to provide better pressure distribution under the lever cap) often takes up too much room to allow chips to pass when the frog is moved forward and the mouth closes down (Figure 3-19). In many cases, both the chipbreaker and the mouth must be relieved before chips will pass. To me, this is just another indication that the frog concept is not a serious effort at solving

the problem of closing down the mouth on a Stanley/Bailey plane. If you experience difficulty with chip clearance when the mouth has a fine setting, I would switch it out for an aftermarket model of the first style.

In the Sta-Set, a new two-part chipbreaker by Clifton, the lower part where the chip is actually broken removes and reinstalls without unscrewing the main body of the chipbreaker from the blade. This is a great timesaver when sharpening. You have to be careful, though, when using waterstones, because water can get between the main body of the chipbreaker and the blade and cause rust. The Sta-Set is rounded, though low, in profile. It fits flat to the blade, rather than arching above it, and is quite a bit thicker than most modern chipbreakers, adding considerable stiffness to the blade (Figure 3-20). Unfortunately it only comes in two widths.

The use of a chipbreaker does introduce some interesting dynamics into the functioning of the blade. With the exception of the Sta-Set, screwing the chipbreaker to the blade firmly enough to ensure tight contact bends the blade into an arc. On wood planes, when used with a heavy, handmade tapered blade fixed with a wedge, this was an advantage. It nearly guaranteed the blade would contact the bed at the heel (right behind the bevel), the most important place, and at the top. This eliminated the need to custom-fit the bed of each plane to the

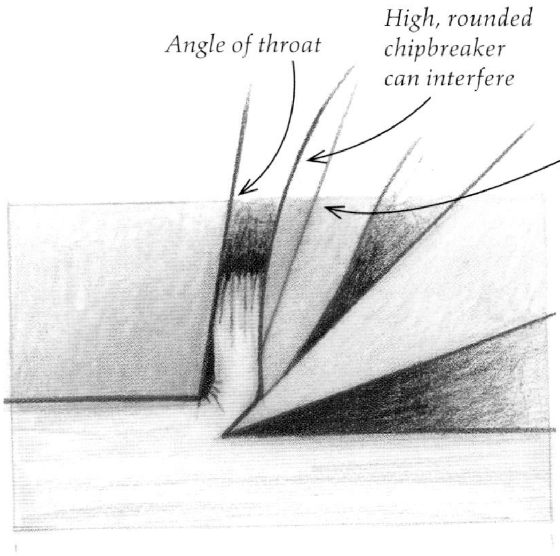

Angle of throat

High, rounded chipbreaker can interfere

Line of flat-bevel chipbreaker

Figure 3-19. *To allow the shaving to pass unobstructed, the throat of the plane should be wider at all points than the thickness of the shaving. On some planes, the high, rounded type of chipbreaker will obstruct the throat.*

Figure 3-20. *The Sta-Set chipbreaker with its edge-piece removed so the blade can be sharpened. Reassembly does not require readjustment, as the part of the chipbreaker that is screwed to the blade has an interlocking groove and a small pin that aligns with a matching hole in the edge piece. The edge piece is then held in place by the lever cap.*

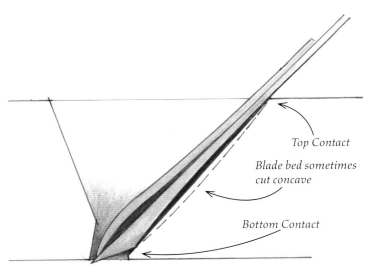

Top Contact

Blade bed sometimes
cut concave

Bottom Contact

Figure 3-21. *Section through an antique wooden plane with a tapered blade*

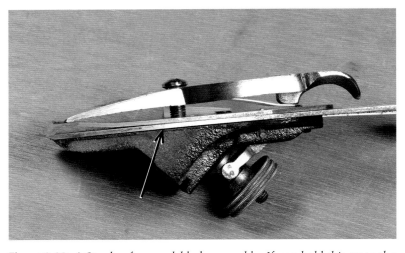

Figure 3-22. *A Stanley frog-and-blade assembly: If you hold this up to the light, you can see that the blade is arched and not making contact with the bed at the center of its length*

varying thickness of the blade and simplified any fine-tuning of the bed. I have even seen the bed of an old plane cut concave to guarantee this fit (Figure 3-21).

I think this strategy relies on a thick blade, assisted by an equally massive chipbreaker. The old tapered blades used on wood planes are nearly ¼" at their thickest part; together with the chipbreaker the assembly is almost ⅜" thick. Contemporary blade/chipbreaker assemblies used on Bailey-style planes together are barely the thickness of an old tapered blade by itself, not much more than ⅛" (3mm). In fact, the thin blade was widely advertised by Stanley as an advantage as there is less to sharpen. The modern Bailey/Stanley chipbreaker appears to be designed to compensate for this lack of blade stiffness with its rounded shape, which seems intended to put pressure on the blade a little farther up as well as on the edge when the lever cap is tightened down. However, it often doesn't work; in many versions, the blade remains arched and is not in full contact with the bed (Figure 3-22).

Using a thin blade not bedded for its full length is just asking for trouble. By itself, it can result in blade chatter. Additionally, if the frog is not carefully seated on the body of the plane, or not aligned with the back edge of the blade opening in the sole, or moved forward to close the mouth, the blade has even less support and could chatter. If your blade chatters, inspect these possible reasons and correct as necessary. If the blade still chatters, try an aftermarket chipbreaker such as Lie-Nielsen, Veritas, or Sta-Set chipbreaker that does not arch the blade when installed, a thicker blade, or both. Be careful when buying a thicker blade, however, because some are too thick to fit into the mouth opening.

Another type of chattering happens because the bevel angle is too small (and thus the blade material immediately behind the edge is too thin). Some woodworkers say the chipbreaker can correct this situation by *pre-tensioning* the cutting edge. However, I would not rely on the chipbreaker to correct for a too-small bevel. It is far better to give the edge its proper bevel angle. (See "Bevel Angle" on page 50.)

SETTING THE CHIPBREAKER

I think the main advantage of the chipbreaker is to increase a plane's versatility. Setting the chipbreaker down close to the edge reduces tearout and allows a more finished cut. Setting the chipbreaker back allows the blade to be more deeply set to hog off wood. All of this can happen regardless of the throat opening, which may be built-in.

How close should the chipbreaker be set to the edge? Generally, the chipbreaker is set back from the edge a distance equal to the maximum thickness of the shaving you expect to make with that plane. This is also usually equal to the amount of curve honed

into the edge of the blade. (See "Shape of the Blade Edge" on page 51). You do not want the chipbreaker set below the corners of the blade. For the finest finish work, I set the chipbreaker down until there is only the barest glint of light left on the top (back) of the blade. This is much less than 1/64" (0.4mm) because only that fine line of light tells me there is still some blade exposed. For the adjustment to work, the chipbreaker must be very well prepared (see "Preparing the Chipbreaker" on page 99) or the chips will jam.

For coarse work, the chipbreaker can be set well back, though it is usually not necessary to set it back much more than 1/16". On planes used to prepare stock, such as the jack, the chipbreaker is usually set back a little more than the arc of the blade edge.

MILLERS FALLS LEVER CAP

The assembly from a Millers Falls plane includes a double-action pivoting lever cap that puts pressure on the blade at three points, flattening out the blade assembly and securely bedding the blade. However, this is exceptional, and I have never seen another lever cap like it.

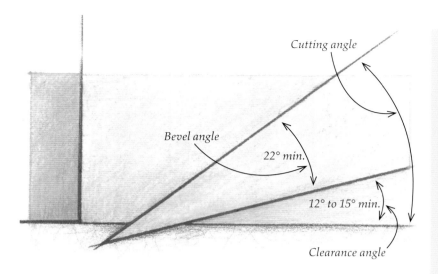

Cutting angle

Bevel angle

22° min.

12° to 15° min.

Clearance angle

Figure 3-23. Practical minimum bevel angle and clearance angle

Bevel Angle

The bevel angle is the angle to which the blade is sharpened. Most blades leave the factory with a 25° or 30° bevel angle. To bring a plane to its finest performance, the bevel angle may well need further attention (Figure 3-23).

If the bevel angle is too small, the edge flexes under the load, bending down until the chip releases, and then springing up to its original position. It may do this repeatedly, resulting in chatter. Or, the blade may flex under the stress of cutting the shaving, especially if it hits a harder part of the board, diving down into the wood and cutting a chip thicker than it was set for. If the plane has a very fine mouth, instead of springing back up, the thicker chip may jam the mouth. Or, the edge can flex under the chipbreaker, opening a gap between the two, which will jam with chips. Therefore, even though the rest of the plane is otherwise finely tuned, the mouth can continue to jam.

As a rule of thumb, the bevel angle should be as small as will cut without chattering. Larger

THE CORRECT BEVEL ANGLE

There are limits and ranges you can use as rules of thumb in correcting the bevel angle. First, the minimum clearance angle on a bevel-down blade should be about 12°, though 15° would be better. The practical lower limit of the bevel for most blades is about 22°—any smaller and the blade usually crumples at the edge in common use. And, as well, some blade steels such as A2 may have trouble giving good service at 25° and smaller bevel angles. Also, the bevel angle varies according to the bedding angle of the blade; the steeper the bedding angle, the greater the bevel angle should be. For instance, a plane with bedding angle of 40° could have a bevel angle of 22°; 25° to 28° would probably be more serviceable; a 45° plane would have a bevel angle of 25° to 30°. A plane with a bedding angle of 55° could have a bevel angle of 30° to 32°, to perhaps as much as 35°. A bedding angle of 65° could have a bevel angle of as much as 38° to 40°.

angles and a restricted mouth opening will place increased stress on the blade edge, causing it to deflect in use. Increasing the bevel angle will alleviate this. The objective is to increase the bevel angle only enough as is required to eliminate chattering. Any more increases resistance and may reduce the smoothness of the cut. Begin with the factory angle and see how it performs. If you suspect it is too small and diagnostic checks (as described in the "Troubleshooting" section on page 125) indicate that is the problem, then increase the bevel angle until achieving the desired performance.

Shape of the Blade Edge

Shaping the blade edge (Figure 3-24) is a traditional technique also not well understood today, but one that greatly increases the effectiveness of the handplane. The basic concept is: roughing and shaping planes have blades of significant curvature across their width; smoothing and finishing planes have blades with decreasing curvature, and the final plane has a nearly straight edge. In theory, on all three planes, the curvature equals to the maximum thickness of the planed shaving (Figure 3-25). The strategy is effective for a number of reasons. On all planes, it keeps the corners of the blade from digging in and tearing up the wood at the borders of the cut. On roughing-out planes properly used diagonally to the grain, it reduces tearout, the amount of effort required to push the plane, and chip jamming at the most likely spot—the corners of the blade. On finish planes, it eliminates steps or ridges between each cut, producing a smoother surface. On jointer planes, the slight curvature can speed up jointing edges and strengthen the resulting edge joint (see "Shooting an Edge" on page 152).

HOW AN EDGE DULLS

To understand why you would want the bevel angle as small as possible, study how an edge dulls. The gradual effect is that the edge rounds over. If the bevel angle is too large, the worn edge retreats from the work and the main bevel begins rubbing, which prevents the edge from contacting the work. This is exacerbated by the natural tendency of the wood to spring back slightly after the cut. The larger the bevel (on a bevel-down blade), the less the clearance angle to the work, and the sooner the action happens.

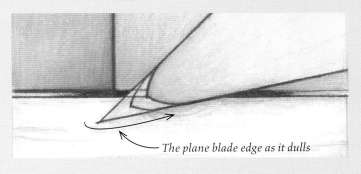

The plane blade edge as it dulls

Figure 3-24. Shape of the Blade Edge

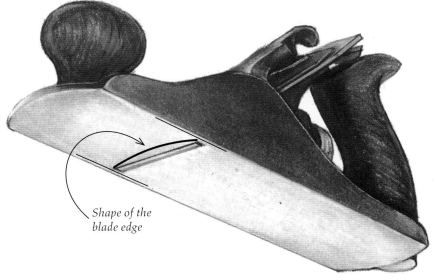

Shape of the blade edge

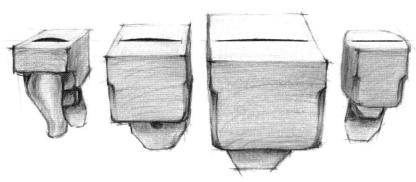

Figure 3-25. *The progression of the curvature of the blades of a set of traditional wood planes, used in order from left to right, rough lumber to smooth. On the far left, the blade of the scrub plane has a curve of ⅛" (3mm) or less; next to it, the jack plane blade has a curve of 1/16" (4mm) or less; the jointer plane blade a curve of 1/32" (0.8mm) or less; and the smoothing plane blade a curve of less than 0.001" (0.025mm).*

A few planes should have a straight edge, most notably rabbet planes. In addition, any plane used on a shooting board should have a blade with a straight edge (see Chapter 10, beginning on page 156).

Length of Plane/ Width of Blade

The length of a plane determines its intended function (Figure 3-26).

Long planes true (straighten) surfaces. Their long length bridges low spots with the blade cutting the high spots down and lowering all surface points to the same plane.

Intermediate-length planes handle initial stock preparation. A longer plane for truing often follows, or they follow a longer plane as a preparatory plane before finish smoothing. Appropriate setup and blade shape accompanies either use (Figure 3-27).

The shortest planes are for final smoothing. They are short for the opposite reason truing planes are long—to follow the low spots. Because of the fine tolerance of their setup and use, variations in the surface of only a few ten-thousandths of an inch may cause the plane to skip over the low spots. On difficult woods, setting the blade deeper to cut to these low spots is not an option because a deeper setting may cause tearout. Shortening the plane's length helps reduce this bridging (Figure 3-28).

A corollary to the length of the plane is the configuration of the bottom of the plane. Western tradition has the bottom of all planes dead flat. However, what is flat?

Figure 3-26. Length of plane determines function

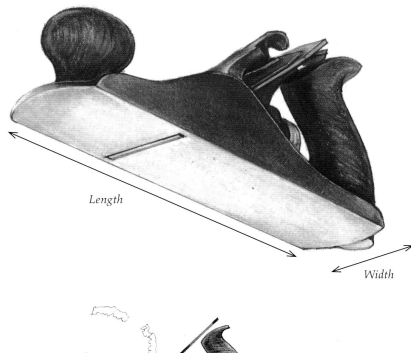

Length

Width

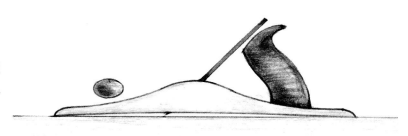

Figure 3-27. *Longer planes bridge the low spots and cut the high spots, giving a truer surface.*

Figure 3-28. *Even though you can see the blade is adjusted to a cutting depth, it may be held off the work and prevented from cutting by the amount the sole is out of true.*

Is within 0.01" (0.25mm) good enough? 0.001" (0.025mm)? 0.0001" (0.0025mm)? In addition, on what areas on the bottom of the plane would the variation be allowed?

The plane needs be only as flat as the finest shaving you expect to make with that plane. If you intend the plane to produce shavings only 9 microns thick, as sometimes happens in Japanese planing competitions, then the bottom of the plane must be within 9 microns of flat; otherwise, the blade may be held off the work by the bottom and will not cut. If you are making a cut ¹⁄₁₆" thick with a jack plane, then the bottom needs to be only less than ¹⁄₁₆" out of flat (though it will work better if it is flatter than that). If you are heading for very fine work, this can be a daunting proposition conceptually;

practically, it is downright frightening. To flatten 20 square inches (or 54 square inches in the case of a #6 foreplane) to within 9 microns, and keep it there, despite wear and variations due to heat and humidity, is meticulous, nearly perpetual work. (See "Configuring the Sole" on page 104 for more on truing soles.)

I follow the lead of the Japanese for a practical answer to flattening the bottom of a plane, one I use on all of my planes. The concept is only three areas minimum need to be in a flat plane, about the width of the blade extending across the sole, and about

HONING A HOLLOW-GROUND BEVEL

An argument against hollow grinding is that it thins the metal immediately behind the edge and produces a bevel angle that is too small. This happens because even though the edge is honed at the proper angle, the steel right behind that honed edge that should support it has been removed—hollowed out to the curve of the grinding wheel. If you

were to draw a tangent to the curve of the grind in the area immediately behind the honed edge, you would see this is a much smaller angle than the honing angle, and could allow the blade to flex. (See Chapter 8 "Sharpening Plane Blades" for a discussion of the types of bevel configurations.)

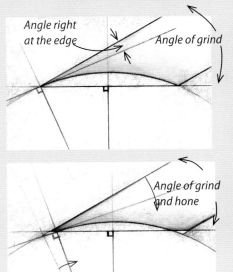

Angle right at the edge

Angle of grind

Tangent to circumference of the hollow grind right behind the edge is the actual support angle, not the grind and hone angle.

Figure 1. *The angle near the edge on a hollow-ground blade (shown here exaggerated for clarity) is much less than the overall angle to which the blade has been ground. On a ³⁄₈"-thick blade, such as a Japanese blade, ground to 30° on a 6"-diameter wheel, the angle is roughly 7° less at the edge than the angle of grind, resulting in about a 23° edge angle—close to the minimum. With a 25° grind, the difference is even greater and results in an edge angle of less than 18°.*

Angle of grind and hone

Angle of support directly behind the edge increases as blade is honed

Figure 2. *As the blade is honed, the hollow decreases with each sharpening, and the angle directly behind the honed edge increases. Eventually, when the bevel has been honed flat, it equals the grind angle.*

Contact areas behind the blade vary in location and number depending on the intended use of the plane.

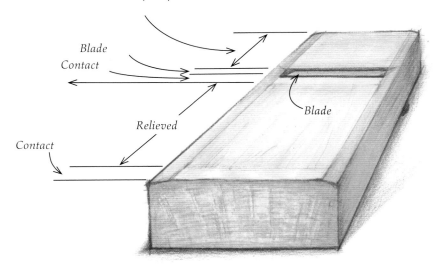

Blade
Contact

Blade

Relieved

Contact

Figure 3-29. *The sole of a Japanese plane is traditionally relieved in strategic areas to simplify maintenance.*

Figure 3-30. *Top, a so-called flat sole may not be contacting the work correctly. Bottom, the sole is relieved to ensure correct contact.*

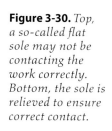

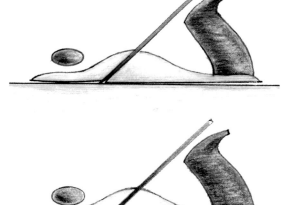

¼" (6mm) long. All other areas are relieved so they do not contact the work or need constant attention (Figure 3-29). This simplifies flattening and maintaining the sole of the plane (Figure 3-30). The contact areas are then configured for the use intended for that particular plane: dimensioning, truing, or smoothing, as the shape of the wood will mirror the way the bottom of the plane is shaped.

To facilitate rapid stock removal, the contact areas of dimensioning planes are relieved in the area following the blade perhaps 0.01" (0.25mm). Truing planes will have all contact areas along the length of the plane in a line, to ensure stock being planed comes out straight. Smoothing planes will have the contact area behind the blade slightly relieved—usually less than the desired thickness of the shaving (approximately 0.005," or 0.125mm)—both to help maintain flatness and to enable a very finely set blade to contact the work. (See the various "Configuring the Sole" sections in Chapter 7.)

The width of the blade (and the plane) also varies according to the intended use of the plane. The blade of the truing plane (the longest plane) also tends to be the widest, traditionally about 2⅜" to 2¾" (60mm to 69mm) wide. This helps produce the flattest surface. Planes for stock preparation, such as the jack, have the narrowest blades, from about 1¼" to 2" (Figure 3-31). Because they are used to remove large amounts of wood, a wide cut would be too much work. Smoothing planes tend to be wider than the stock-removal planes, but just how wide is pretty much up to the crafter. The wider the blade, the less pronounced the faint scallops, which are a result of the faint curvature of the blade edge. However, a wider blade involves more setup, maintenance, and work to use. Smoothing planes, especially for hardwood, are in the range of 2" to 2⅜" wide.

AND REMEMBER...

There is an additional aspect of effective plane work that tends to be overlooked—the sharpness of the blade. No planing operation will be very effective unless the blade is sharp. This becomes unavoidably apparent during demanding finish-planing operations. While you can continue to push a dull plane with increasing effort and increasing tearout when roughing down a board (the change is so gradual, the blade often is dull before you notice it), on a demanding finish-planing operation, unless the plane is exquisitely sharp, results will be immediately disappointing—no waiting.

Beginners often find sharpness difficult to judge. It is often a fleeting thing, seemingly there one moment and gone the next. As your woodworking skills grow, you will become more demanding of your tools and accept only true sharpness. You will learn that some blades do not get as sharp as others. There are nuances of difference in the concept of sharp. Without a blade sharp enough for the task, however, all other strategies for effective planing fail.

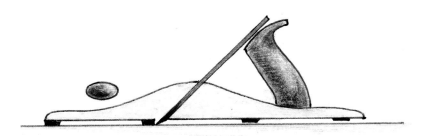

Figure 3-31. *The jack plane may have its sole slightly relieved behind the blade to facilitate access to a rough surface when first preparing a board. See Figure 7-22 on page 110.*

THE PROPORTION OF LENGTH TO WIDTH

In traditional wood planes, truing planes range in length from about 18" to 30" (450mm to 760mm). Both preparation and intermediate smoothing planes range in length from about 13" to 18" (330mm to 460mm). Smoothing planes range in length anywhere from 6" to 12" (150mm to 300mm).

In the Bailey-style of iron plane, the truing planes are the #7 and #8, 22" and 24" respectively. Preparation planes are the #5 (14" long) and often the #6 (18" long), which is used before the #7 or #8. The wider #5 ½ and sometimes the #6 are usually for intermediate smoothing. The #3, #4, and #4 ½ are used for smoothing, while the wider #4 ½ is often the final plane used in smoothing.

None of this is set in stone, however. It is up to the crafter to decide the best use for planes of particular lengths and widths.

HOW FLAT IS "FLAT"

One of the rationales for development of the metal plane is it comes out of the box flat and is easier to keep flat, although anyone who has tried to flatten a metal plane knows neither is true. The end user can go to great lengths to ensure the entire bottom of a plane is flat to within 6 thousandths of an inch. Practically speaking, this is a backbreaking proposition, and a great obstacle to properly setting up a handplane. Even with a milling machine, true flatness is hard to achieve, as the necessary clamping process often distorts the plane, so when it is removed from the clamps it springs back, out of true. However, it is also a maintenance problem. Just like wood, iron moves. It needs to age for at least six months after casting so the cast-in stresses can relax. It still moves, albeit a lot less, for quite a time after that. Additionally, various stresses can cause it to move, not the least of which would be if dropped. However, even the constant pressure of the cap-iron screw can distort the body. In addition, it wears. While it may wear more slowly than wood, it just takes that much more effort to flatten it.

4

ANATOMY

Understanding How the
Stanley/Bailey Plane Works

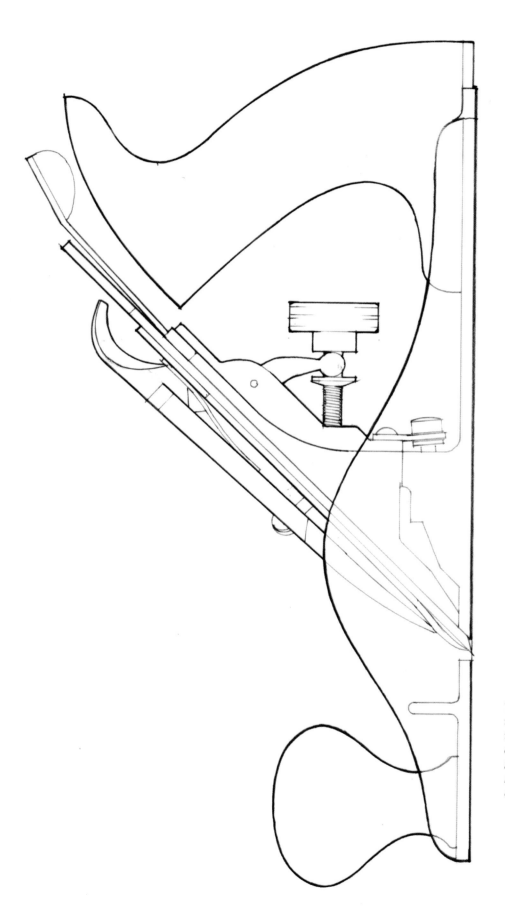

The Bailey plane uses the same anatomical tactics as any other plane, but its innovative adjustment mechanisms are different from all others.

For someone just starting out in woodworking, and even for the experienced professional, the all-metal plane developed by Leonard Bailey in 1869 will be the easiest to set up and maintain, and will give the most predictable results of all the different planes available. Some styles of planes may give better results for some of the tasks a plane is asked to do, but for all around versatility the metal plane is hard to beat (Figure 4-1).

The toolmaker Leonard Bailey first patented his plane in 1867, the result of at least 9 years of work. Though his patent shows a plane with a wood base, it has many features we would recognize today: a cammed lever cap, a thin parallel (e.g. non-tapered) blade, a knob front handle and open rear handle, a nut-and-fork blade adjuster, a moveable blade bed, and a metal frame for mounting it all. By 1869 he had developed the all-metal plane. He sold his company and patent rights to Stanley Tool Works in 1869 and Stanley has been producing it since. The company made a number of minor improvements over the years, but the tool has remained basically unchanged since 1910.

TWO TYPES

The metal planes designed by Leonard Bailey and produced by the Stanley Tool Works (and many others) are of two broad types: those with the blade mounted bevel down and those with the blade mounted bevel up. The vast

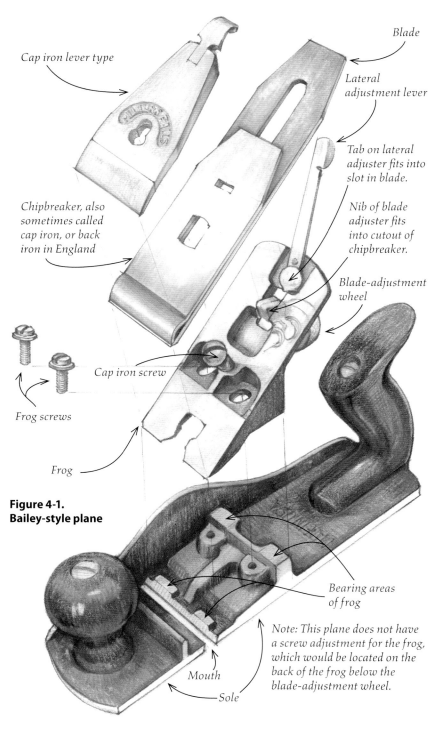

Cap iron lever type

Blade

Lateral adjustment lever

Tab on lateral adjuster fits into slot in blade.

Chipbreaker, also sometimes called cap iron, or back iron in England

Nib of blade adjuster fits into cutout of chipbreaker.

Blade-adjustment wheel

Cap iron screw

Frog screws

Frog

Bearing areas of frog

**Figure 4-1.
Bailey-style plane**

Note: This plane does not have a screw adjustment for the frog, which would be located on the back of the frog below the blade-adjustment wheel.

Mouth

Sole

majority of planes made by Stanley Tool Works
were planes with the blade mounted bevel
down, much like most of its wood predecessors.
They made these in all the bench plane sizes
plus many more specialty planes. Planes made
with the blade mounted bevel up were mostly
limited to the small block planes (#60½, #9½),
miter planes, some specialty planes, and the #62
and #64, planes the size of the jack plane that
are now being reproduced by Lie-Nielsen and
Lee Valley. The wide range of sizes we have now
is a recent phenomenon.

The Bevel-Down Planes

The Bailey plane (Figure 4-2) (or the Stanley/
Bailey plane, or the Stanley plane—and I'll
probably refer to it by any one of those labels
throughout), are distinguished by, among other
things, their all-metal construction and their
adjustable blade bed (or "frog") that screws to
the sole. All of the makes of bevel-down Stanley
planes, with one recent exception, have this
feature. The frog has always been advertised as
a way to adjust the mouth opening, a feature
that greatly increases the plane's versatility.
Adjusting the mouth opening allows the
plane to be used both for fine smoothing, by
closing the mouth down; and for removing
large amounts of wood, by opening the mouth
up. On my little block plane (bevel-up) I will
often adjust the mouth opening several times

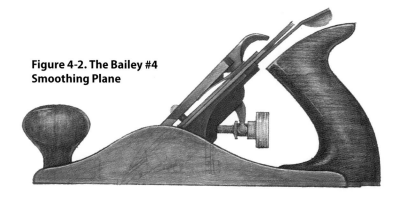

Figure 4-2. The Bailey #4 Smoothing Plane

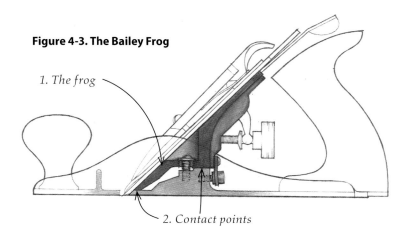

Figure 4-3. The Bailey Frog

1. The frog

2. Contact points

a day as I use it to do different tasks. But
unfortunately, the frog on the bevel-down
Bailey plane is clumsy to adjust and I've always
felt that this type of blade bed was done mostly
to accommodate casting and manufacturing
procedures.

THE FROG

There are two (Figure 4-3) traditional types
of frogs, and a couple of new ones. The original
type designed by Bailey has two to four small
bearing points on two levels milled on its

underside that mate with matching points milled on the upper side of the sole. It is fixed to the sole with screws through slotted holes that allow it to be adjusted forward or backward. This allows the user to adjust the width of the mouth opening. This is not a truly successful solution to the problem of finding a way to close the mouth down, as when the frog is moved forward out of alignment with the edge of the sole below it, it leaves the blade unsupported (Figure 4-4); on some planes for nearly ¼". On the original models, when this is combined with a blade that might not be much thicker than ¹⁄₁₆" and a thin sheet metal chipbreaker, the blade is prone to chatter when asked to do any serious work. A thicker blade can be substituted, but many times an aftermarket blade will actually be too thick to fit into the mouth—even though it looks as if you would have plenty of room.

Additionally, in order to adjust the frog, you have to remove the blade to loosen the frog screws, reinstall it to get the position you want, pull it off again to tighten the frog screws, and then put it back on again—so you're not going to be doing it very often. (Figure 4-5).

A better solution is the "Bedrock" style frog (Figure 4-6). This style of frog is found on Stanley's Bedrock planes manufactured from around 1900 until the early 1940s and recently reintroduced by a number of premium makers. The frog itself is wedge-shaped and sits on a sloped ramp milled into

Figure 4-4. *Moving the frog forward on a Stanley-style plane to close the mouth will leave the edge unsupported—on some models by nearly ¼" (6mm).*

Figure 4-5. *The screw adjusts the frog forward or backward. You have to remove the blade and chipbreaker to loosen the screws that allow it to work (unlike the Bedrock), but without accurately milled ways to run on, you can't count on the frog maintaining a parallel position when adjusted. Your best technique is to retighten the screws that hold the frog down just enough that the frog doesn't rock, but still can be adjusted and then reinstall the blade/ chipbreaker and adjust the frog until you have the mouth opening you want. Then remove the blade and chiobreaker, tighten down the frog screws (not too much) and then put the blade back in. There is considerable slop in the adjuster so you also cannot count on the frog returning to its exact position once it has been loosened. Also, there is little room for your hand and no room at all for a full-size screwdriver to get in to use the adjustment screw (using a screwdriver with a long shank to clear the handle is your best bet).*

Figure 4-6. The Bedrock Frog

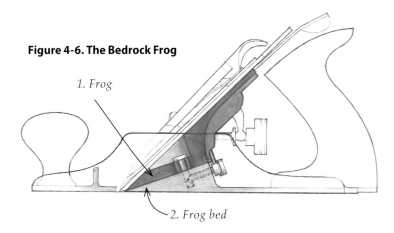

1. Frog

2. Frog bed

the top of the sole. The tapered frog and ramp allows the blade to be fully supported regardless of its position. Even better, you don't have to disassemble the blade to adjust it. The frog is held down by an ingenious tapered pin-in-socket method that allows you to adjust the frog by loosening two set-screws and then using an adjuster screw to move the frog.

Not totally ingenious, however. Because the frog moves down as it moves forward on its ramp, the blade's depth must also be continually readjusted back to its functioning depth in order to correctly gauge the size of the mouth opening. This means there is still a lot of trial and error, tightening, loosening, moving until you get it right. Also, some versions have no method to keep the frog aligned with the plane, and so you also have to check to make sure the frog hasn't twisted on its seat. It's easier than the original Bailey design, but still not something that you want to do frequently should you want to increase the versatility of the plane.

Traditionally, all frogs were manufactured to provide a blade angle of 45°. But recently, Lie-Nielsen has brought out frogs in 50° and 55° that can be interchanged in some of their planes; and Lee Valley will make frogs in ½° increments from 40° to 65° to your order for use in their customizable planes. Blade angle has been one of the most difficult things to customize as it is built in, but the serendipitous use of a removable frog has

allowed the development of custom angles and greatly increased the versatility of these planes. Now you can buy just a frog if you wish, instead of a whole plane, for those occasions when a high blade angle would be useful. Of course you have to own one of these planes to begin with (not cheap). And most likely you'll have to have a second blade and chipbreaker assembly with a modified bevel edge and chipbreaker edge geometry to accommodate the steeper angle. Interestingly, on the Lee Valley, the frog does not adjust: they utilize a moveable mouthpiece to adjust the mouth (Figure 4-7).

Figure 4-7. *Veritas Custom Bench Planes uses a Bedrock-style frog that is available in ½° increments from 40° to 65°. The plane uses an adjustable mouth, rather than a movable frog.*

Figure 4-8. *Veritas Bench Planes uses a different type of frog developed by the manufacturer. It allows the mouth opening to be adjusted without removing the blade assembly and fully supports the blade in all positions.*

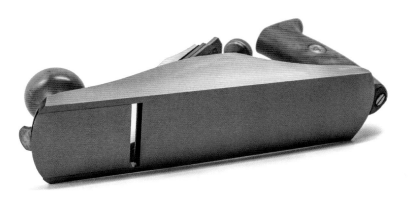

Figure 4-9. *Stanley's new Sweetheart #4 bench plane has a solid frog. It uses an adjustable mouth plate to adjust the mouth opening.*

A third type of frog has been introduced by Lee Valley. This frog protrudes through the plane and is flush to the sole right behind the blade, giving the blade good support. It rests on milled ways and extends back to include the handle (Figure 4-8). It is adjustable without removing the blade or resetting it. An innovation by Lee Valley, this frog would seem to solve all difficulties of the use of a frog to adjust the mouth opening, though you still have to use a screwdriver and it only comes in a 45° pitch. But perhaps using a moveable frog to adjust the mouth opening is not the best approach?

Just recently Stanley itself has brought out its Sweetheart line of hand planes. Their solution to a way to close the mouth is to use a moveable mouthpiece, similar to what's done in a bevel-up plane. The bevel-down bench plane in the series (a #4) has this adjustable mouthpiece and uses an integral, non-adjustable cast-in blade-bed at 45°. While such a contrast in density of cast iron might result in additional movement of the casting over time, possibly affecting the flatness of the sole, it does make for a solid blade bed (Figure 4-9).

The Adjusters

THE BAILEY ADJUSTER

One of Leonard Bailey's big innovations was the nut-and-fork adjuster: rotating a knurled wheel behind the blade moved a pivoted forked lever with a nib on the other end of it that engaged a slot in the chipbreaker screwed to the blade—and thus moved the blade (Figure 4-10).

The goal of a good adjuster is to be able to move the blade accurately with little or no backlash (slop) and to be able to do it with the blade under sufficient pressure to keep it from losing its adjustment.

The Bailey adjuster is quite good at being able to adjust the blade while under working pressure. Backlash is a different story. By its very design, backlash is inherent. I've had planes that took two plus turns of the wheel before the blade was engaged and if you over adjusted it, it took two-plus turns back to begin to change it. That's a lot of spinning. And then sometimes if you didn't return the wheel to a position that put downward pressure on the blade to keep it from backing out under the pressure of the cut, the blade would slip its adjustment.

This arrangement also requires the use of a second, lateral adjuster. Not a problem really, except that using it could affect the blade's depth, requiring some additional wheel spinning. The best-made Bailey adjuster will have only a little more than a quarter turn to engage the cutter; but lateral adjustment may still affect the depth setting.

The Bailey adjuster, however, does excel at being able to adjust the blade depth on the fly by using the first finger on the wheel while gripping the handle. You must be close to your setting to do this, and the adjuster traveling in the same direction as the needed adjustment. Otherwise you will have to back the adjuster off several turns and start over, requiring the use of two fingers if not two hands.

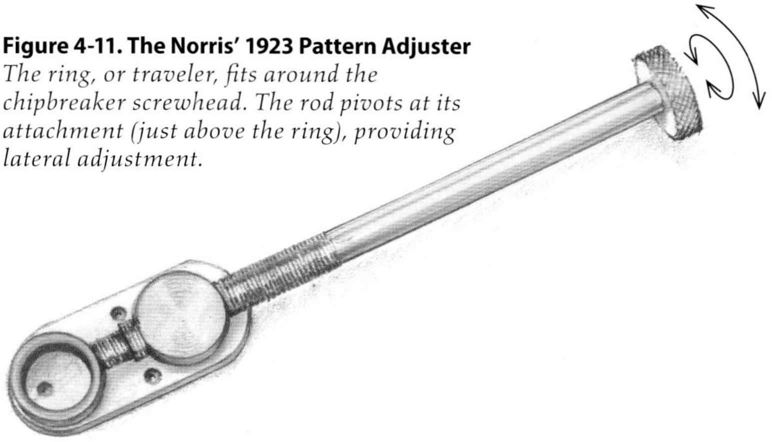

THE NORRIS ADJUSTER

The Norris adjuster (Figure 4-11) was patented by Thomas Norris, a London planemaker, in 1913 and improved in 1923, and continued to be used on his planes until he ceased production in 1940. Unlike the Bailey adjuster, which requires the use of a second device for lateral adjustment, the Norris adjuster performs both depth adjustment and lateral adjustment: the

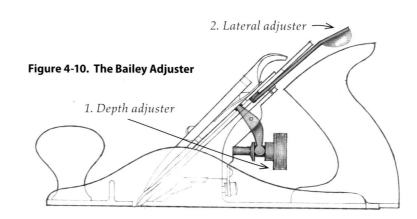

2. Lateral adjuster

Figure 4-10. The Bailey Adjuster

1. Depth adjuster

Figure 4-11. The Norris' 1923 Pattern Adjuster
The ring, or traveler, fits around the chipbreaker screwhead. The rod pivots at its attachment (just above the ring), providing lateral adjustment.

adjustment rod is threaded through a fixed pivot point and is reverse-threaded to a ring that fits around the chipbreaker screw. Turning the adjustment rod advances or retreats the the ring around the chipbreaker screw. Moving the lever left or right provides lateral adjustment.

The Norris-style adjuster is a fine performer, inherently more accurate and intuitive than the Bailey adjuster. When finely machined its accuracy is exceeded only by the Primus adjuster on the German wood Primus planes, which unfortunately is not available on any Bailey type plane (the Primus adjuster is under the tension of a strong spring which effectively eliminates backlash). Even when a Norris adjuster's machining is only mediocre I've rarely seen an adjuster with more than a half turn of play, far less than a Bailey adjuster of similar quality and almost as good as the most finely made Bailey.

But there is a problem with the Norris adjuster: it has difficulty adjusting the blade when it is under the full working pressure of the cap iron. Ideally, the pressure on the cap iron should be backed off a little when adjusting the blade. Many old Norris planes are found with the threads of their adjusters stripped because the worker continued to adjust the plane under full pressure. Continuing to adjust the blade under full pressure on a new plane will wear the threads on the adjuster prematurely, causing increasing backlash as it wears.

This is why you will usually see a screw-down cap iron on a plane with a Norris adjuster. The lever cap found on the Bailey plane is adjusted once with a screwdriver and only readjusted occasionally. It is quicker to set and release: the screw-down cap tends to squiggle around when first tightening the screw, and takes a few turns to complete, unlike the snap of a lever cap.

LATERAL ADJUSTMENT

Bailey's lateral adjustment is a lever pivoted on the frog that extends above the top of the blade. It has a disk or bent tab on the lower end that engages the screw slot in the blade. (see Figure 4-1 on page 58) Moving the lever left or right changes the angle of the blade left to right and thus the blade edge to the work.

The Norris adjuster works in a similar manner, though since it is usually attached lower down on the blade (to the chipbreaker screw), it is less effective and a bit indeterminate. To overcome this, modern makers have provided set-screws either side of the blade down near the edge, ostensibly to keep the blade aligned, but really as a pivot point for lateral adjustment.

CAP IRON

Part of Bailey's innovation was the lever cap, a cap iron for clamping the blade down to keep it from losing its adjustment when used. It replaced the wedge, which was the common way to fix the blade, even on iron bodied planes. But better than that, it could be installed with the snap of a lever. Very quick.

The second type of cap iron is tightened with a screw. These are used either for economy or, as in the case of the Norris adjusters, so that pressure can be backed off to allow adjustment of the blade.

Stanley/Bailey planes almost always had the lever cap, though some other makers would use a screw cap, most notably Record in their last years of making handplanes, and many modern makers for either economy or ease of adjustment.

BLADES

Blades run the gamut, from pretty fine to miserable. They are traditionally thin, parallel (i.e., not tapered as were many blades for wooden planes) and until World War II, laminated with a hard edge-steel backed with a softer backing steel. These features were all among Leonard Bailey's innovations. The claim was that since the blade was thin there was less steel to remove when sharpening, and so sharpening went faster; even better, only part of that steel was hard steel, making it easier yet. These blades are pretty good performers.

But when buying secondhand, you can't count on the blade in the plane being the one that came with the plane, or as even being contemporary to the plane. After the war, a variety of steels were used at different periods with different manufacturers—with generally indifferent results. Some of these were marked with the type of steel they were and some were not. Record was at one point marking their blades tungsten vanadium; they were OK for general carpentry but not for fine work.

And the thin blade could be problematic. As time went on, the thin blade became more of an opportunity to reduce costs (maybe it always was!). A shift in the market toward power tools for the professional and hand tools for the homeowner and hobbyist allowed the blade to be downgraded. It also resulted in design changes that prevented the blade from being well supported, allowing it to chatter.

Modern upmarket versions of the Bailey plane usually use a significantly thicker blade than the original planes did, as well as blade beds of significant area, and tight-fitting chipbreakers held down with a well-designed cap iron that applies well-distributed pressure. This seems to be effective in preventing chatter (Figure 4-12).

Figure 4-12. *At the bottom of the photo is the typical blade/chipbreaker assembly found in vintage Stanley/Bailey planes, with its bulbous chipbreaker and thin blade. In the middle is an after-market assembly typical of the high-end Bailey plane manufacturers. At top is a tapered blade from an antique wooden plane, mounted with a Sta-Set chipbreaker. Notice the difference in thickness of not only the entire assemblies, but also of the blades themselves.*

CHIPBREAKER

The Stanley-style chipbreaker is singular in design. Its distinctive shape is intended to distribute the pressure from the lever cap's two pressure points to keep the blade flat to the bed and thus prevent chattering.

It doesn't always work. What's more, in some designs the pronounced hump interferes with being able to close the mouth to a fine setting. (See Chapter 3 for more on chipbreakers).

CORRUGATIONS

A sole with grooves cut into it is intended to reduce resistance when pushing the plane. I think at one time some of the catalogs advertised that this is because of reduced friction (not correct according to the laws of physics, I've been told). But apparently, there is increased resistance as the surface of the wood more closely matches that of the sole of the plane as it is planed, a kind of "suction." It's rather minimal, though it might be more important if you intend to use your plane for extended periods. It does represent less iron that has to be removed when the sole has to be tuned up, but then sometimes the corrugations can hang up on narrow stock. As you can see, the argument for or against the corrugated sole is not strong; I usually try and get the corrugated version of the plane if I can—partially because I think these were made for a professional demographic and thus tend to be better quality—but it's a matter of personal taste.

Regardless of whether the sole is corrugated or not, the sole of an iron plane should be lubricated in use. The surface resistance of an iron sole is significantly higher than that of a wood plane; lubricating the sole greatly reduces the effort required to push the plane. A candle or some paraffin wax could be squiggled down the sole periodically. Or a benchtop oiler using camelia oil can be made. The edges of a corrugated sole tend to hold a little extra wax—another (weak) argument for the corrugated sole!

HANDLES

The knob and open tote (or handle) of the Bailey plane is virtually its signature. This has not significantly changed since Day One. In 1922 the knob went from somewhat squat and mushroom-shaped to taller and

THE OILER

For all styles of planes and planing, it is helpful to have a large oiler sitting on the bench. Drag the sole of the plane over it (backward) periodically while working, to keep the sole of the plane—and the blade edge as well—lubricated while working. This allows planing rhythm to be virtually uninterrupted.

The oiler should be around 3" in diameter: a lidded canister, a drilled out block of wood, or, traditionally, a large bamboo knuckle. Rip rags to about 3" or 4" (76mm or 102mm) wide. It will take the better part of a bed sheet. Wrap the rags continuously in a coil until you reach the desired diameter—usually slightly larger than the hole it is to go into. Wrap the end to be inserted with heavy plastic such as a plastic drop cloth or Visqueen, and work the whole roll into the hole. About ½" (13mm) or more of the cloth should protrude from the container; cut the plastic off even with the container. Saturate the cloth with camellia oil (available at Japanese tools suppliers), which provides light, contaminate-free lubrication.

Two oilers, both made from a section of bamboo. *The larger one is about 3" (76mm) in diameter and sits on the bench when used. Take the plane to the oiler and stroke its sole over it during planing as part of the rhythm of work. The smaller one is about 1½" (38mm) in diameter and is picked up to be used.*

rounder, but beyond that, little has changed. Some post-WWII planes had their handles slightly "streamlined," and some modern manufacturers pay more attention to trying to achieve a modernized line at the sacrifice of comfort and working efficiency, but the signature remains.

Many people will find the handles blistering if they have to use the plane for extended periods of heavy planing. Smoothing the slot and other edges of the front knob screw will avert one blister. Many times the angle of the rear handle is not right (and it may be too small) causing the little finger and side of the hand to push repeatedly against the handle's bottom. Some handle shapes will chafe the web between the thumb and first finger, mostly because the handle doesn't have enough curve to engage the entire hand. But handles can be retrofitted.

BLADE LOCATION

A note should be made as to the location of the blade along the length of the plane. Stanley planes were always made with the blade about one-third the length of the plane back from its leading edge, regardless of the length of the plane. On the shorter planes it's obvious that this is done to be able to fit the frog mechanism and rear handle, which take a minimum amount of room, regardless of the length of the plane. This is not a problem, but it differs from many other styles of planes which have their blades more centrally located (in some cases very centrally located). It requires a bit more concentration when beginning the cut, especially on the shorter

planes. Recently, Lee Valley has moved its blades to a slightly more central point on some of its planes.

The Bevel-Up Planes

Until recently, the only bevel-up bench planes (Figure 4-13) commonly available were the little Stanley #60½ and #9½ block planes—carpenter's favorites. For a while Stanley also made the #62, a 14"-long plane with an adjustable mouth that was advertised as being designed for heavy work across the grain; and the #64, the same size but without the adjustable mouth, that was used to resurface end grain butcher blocks. Both of these were discontinued around World War II.

However, with the recent renaissance of planemaking the utility and versatility of the bevel-up style of plane have been reassessed. The versatility of the design is probably unexcelled; it can go from hogging off large amounts of wood to taking transparently thin shavings, often with little tearout, in

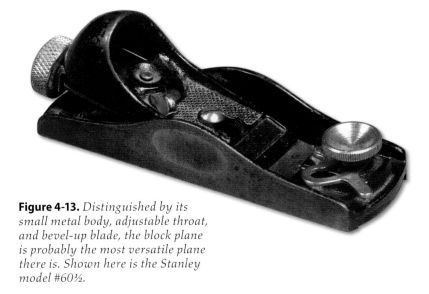

Figure 4-13. *Distinguished by its small metal body, adjustable throat, and bevel-up blade, the block plane is probably the most versatile plane there is. Shown here is the Stanley model #60½.*

Figure 4-14. *In this photo you can see three of the different adjustment mechanisms used in different versions of the 60 ½. From left to right: Stanley, Veritas, and Lie-Nielsen. The Stanley uses a stamped metal traveler with a nib on it that fits into one of a series of notches in the underside of the blade; the traveler is attached to a threaded rod. The lateral adjuster is possibly the easiest of the three to use. The Veritas uses a variation of the Norris adjuster that fits into one of two holes in the blade. The Lie-Nielsen uses a thread rod with a flange that fits into a slot in the underside of the blade. It has no lateral adjuster, per se. The Stanley and Lie-Nielsen have an eccentric cam lever to adjust the mouth opening that makes it much eaier to adjust than just a knob.*

seconds. Because the blade is mounted bevel up, changing the bevel angle by regrinding or honing a secondary bevel will change the cutting angle; this can result in tearout-free surfaces in difficult woods.

The construction of the plane is simpler than the bevel-down planes; with the low bed angle (12° to 13.5°) there is no room for a frog. The adjuster is simpler too, usually a variation on the Norris adjuster where a threaded rod moves a traveler that fits into a notch or hole in the blade. Method of lateral adjustment varies. Veritas uses the same

threaded rod that adjusts the depth, similar to the original Norris. Stanley has a patented lever with tabs that fits up into the slot cut into the blade. Ironically, the most expensive version of the plane has no lateral adjustment mechanism: the blade is adjusted laterally by actually pushing the blade left or right after loosening the blade clamp (Figure 4-14).

At this time, more than one manufacturer makes a bevel-up version of a full size smoother, a jack (similar to the Stanley #62) and a jointer plane, and there are a multitude of versions of the little block plane as well.

These planes are excellent for miscellaneous work around the shop: trimming, smoothing edges and ends, chamfering. I use my block plane frequently throughout the day, often changing the blade setting and mouth opening back and forth for both heavy and fine, smooth cuts (Figure 4-15).

So why hasn't everyone made the transition to bevel-up planes?

The plane can be a little problematic when used as a bench plane for preparing large, difficult surfaces. It is a plane without a chipbreaker, relying totally on the compression provided by a tight mouth opening to control tearout. With a bed angle of only 12° and a bevel angle of 25° to 30° the resulting cutting angle is only 37° to 42°— quite low for planing hardwoods and an angle that often results in disastrous tearout. If you're preparing stock by making a deep cut and trying to minimize tearout by tightening down the mouth, you're putting a lot of pressure on the edge, causing quite a bit of heat that will degrade the edge quite quickly. Grinding and honing a higher bevel angle can achieve a more appropriate cutting angle. So for instance, if you want to plane walnut and want to use a cutting angle of 55°, you can grind a bevel angle of 43°, which when combined with the bed angle of 12° gives a cutting angle of 55°. But 43° is a pretty blunt bevel angle that will have lots of resistance in cutting and will generate plenty of heat— and heat will cause a cutting edge to degrade

pretty quickly. Using the plane you're going to have greater resistance in pushing, reduced clarity in the surface from the blunt angle, and more frequent sharpening.

All of this is fine if you only have to do it occasionally, or if it pulls you out of a difficult situation, but doing considerable work like this will be inefficient and eventually frustrating.

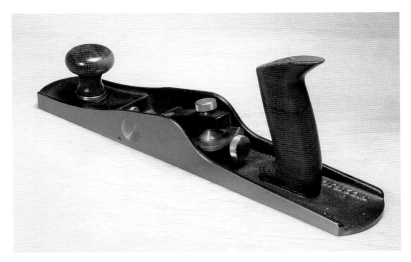

Figure 4-15. *The Lie Nielsen and (above) the Veritas low-angle jack are versatile planes suitable for many of the tasks around the shop.*

5

BENCH PLANES

Traditional Solutions: the Jack, Jointer, and Smoothing Planes

Bench planes perform three basic functions in woodworking: shaping and dimensioning lumber, truing and preparing pieces for gluing, and smoothing surfaces. The correct application of the anatomical tactics discussed in Chapter 3 is critical to effectively performing these tasks. Because each task requires a significantly different combination of tactics, traditionally a different plane was developed and used for each: the jack, the jointer, and the smoothing plane. They are visually distinguished from each other primarily by their length relative to the width of their blade and by the shape of the blade's edge. Varying other tactics also maximize work efficiency.

*A set of Bailey bench planes:
#5 Jack, #7 Jointer, and #4
Smoothing. Collection of
Alan R. Garner.*

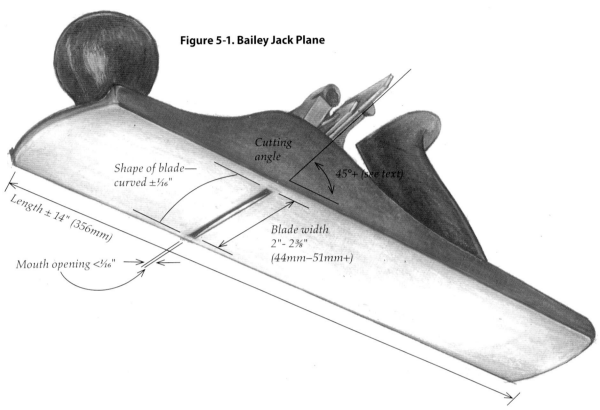

Figure 5-1. Bailey Jack Plane

Cutting angle

45°+ *(see text)*

Shape of blade—curved ±¹⁄₁₆"

Blade width 2"- 2⅜" (44mm–51mm+)

Length ± 14" (356mm)

Mouth opening <¹⁄₁₆"

I informally call these three types of planes the *triumvirate*—from the old Roman phrase meaning, "the three who jointly rule." Additional planes assist these and fill various particular needs. However, these three planes are basic and, for centuries, have formed the core of the broad spectrum of handplanes. While you may only rarely dimension lumber or true an edge with handplanes, understanding the form and anatomy of the jack, jointer, and smoother and how they have traditionally worked allows you to effectively select, use, and modify handplanes in your own work.

The Jack Plane

Most closely identified with shaping and dimensioning lumber is the jack plane (Figure 5-1). It is traditionally used to remove a fair amount of wood quickly to bring a piece to rough shape and dimension after being rough-sawn, split, or hewn from the log. It usually is in the neighborhood of 14" (356mm) long, this slightly longer length aiding in the initial straightening and leveling of stock from the rough. For rapid stock removal, and to reduce tearout and resistance, the edge of the blade sharpens to a curve, projecting as much as ¹⁄₁₆" (2mm) (Figure 5-2).

The chipbreaker is set well back from the edge—a minimum of ¹⁄₁₆" (2mm). It serves to engage the blade-adjustment mechanism more than to reduce tearout. (Figure 5-3). In addition, to minimize effort in using the plane, the blade is narrow, about 1¾" (44mm) up to 2¼" (57mm). Traditionally, in jack planes the blade angle is set at the lowest angle among the three planes of the triumvirate; as low as 40°, though 43° or 45° is more common. The sole is configured straight or slightly convex over its length, with the contact area behind the blade relieved perhaps 0.01" (0.25mm). Because this is a rough plane and makes a deep cut, maintenance of a flat bottom is less critical.

The jack is a real workhorse. Before the common availability of power tools, the jack did the bulk of the dimensioning and surfacing in the woodshop, often resulting in being knee-deep in shavings by lunchtime. Except when working on edges and narrow pieces, the plane is pushed across the grain diagonally *with the grain* (not *into* it). This results in the curved blade making a nice *downhill* shearing cut with the grain, reducing both effort and tearout in all but the most difficult-grained woods.

The jack plane is the one we all start with, in our tool kit as well as at the bench. We commonly purchase and use a single plane

for a long time to shape, dimension, and smooth work—the job of the jack. As your skills improve, you become more demanding and look for more specialized tools to address specific tasks. Nevertheless, the traditional use of the jack in the multi-step process of stock preparation remains relevant. Stock that is too large for your equipment need not intimidate you. Proper use of the jack and the others in the triumvirate makes such work go

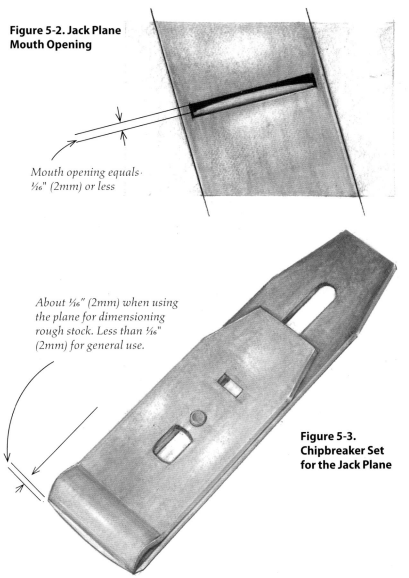

Figure 5-2. Jack Plane Mouth Opening

Mouth opening equals ¹⁄₁₆" (2mm) or less

About ¹⁄₁₆" (2mm) when using the plane for dimensioning rough stock. Less than ¹⁄₁₆" (2mm) for general use.

Figure 5-3. Chipbreaker Set for the Jack Plane

quickly. In addition, understanding the jack allows you to choose aspects of its anatomy for customizing other planes for other purposes. If you know why the blade curves, for instance, you can decide whether your use requires a blade with curvature, and if so, how much. Or perhaps have another blade with a different curvature for other tasks. From experience with the jack, you can reference how big a throat opening or chipbreaker setback, or what sole configuration, another plane requires. You can modify planes of different sizes for shaping or preparing pieces not going through the jointer or planer. Your work becomes faster, more efficient, and not limited by your power tools—only by your imagination, resourcefulness, and willingness to experiment.

The jack plane should be light because you will be lifting and moving it a lot. It should be easy on the hands, capable of hard work without causing blisters, and have a low coefficient of friction. For all of these reasons, the Bailey plane would generally not be your first choice if this was all you were to use it for. Traditionally, a wooden plane is often preferred; but since few woodworkers today do much serious stock preparation with handplanes, you can save buying the wood jack until you really need it. The Bailey plane does a fine job of prepping stock; a good wood jack just makes it easier.

THE FORE PLANE

In a time when most stock was prepared by hand, another plane was also often used: the fore plane, 14" to 17" (356mm to 432mm) long (this correlates with the Stanley #6). It was often set up like a jack plane, with significant curvature to the blade, and was generally used to prepare larger stock or rough down a long edge in preparation for shooting it with the jointer or long plane. Its actual setup would vary with the craftsman's particular needs. The fore plane could also be followed by the try plane, about 22" (559mm) long and used to prepare an edge for trial fitting (thus its name) before being finally shot true with the jointer or long plane

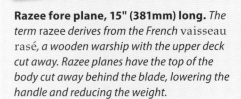

Razee fore plane, 15" (381mm) long. *The term* razee *derives from the French* vaisseau rasé, *a wooden warship with the upper deck cut away. Razee planes have the top of the body cut away behind the blade, lowering the handle and reducing the weight.*

Figure 5-4. Bailey Jointer Plane. Traditional Western Wooden Jointer Plane

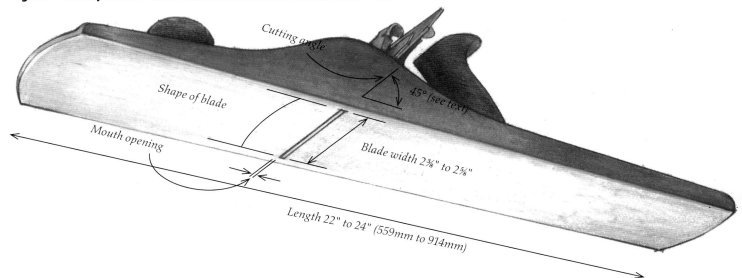

Cutting angle

45° (see text)

Shape of blade

Mouth opening

Blade width 2⅜" to 2⅝"

Length 22" to 24" (559mm to 914mm)

TRYING, LONG, AND JOINTER

We classify any plane 20" to 30" long as a jointer plane. Up until about the 1870s, however, three distinct planes occupied this range: the trying (or try) plane, 20" to 22" long; the long plane, 24" to 26" long; and the jointer plane, 28" to 30" long. After 1870, use of these planes began to diminish, as did the distinction between them.

Figure 5-5. Jointer Plane Mouth Opening

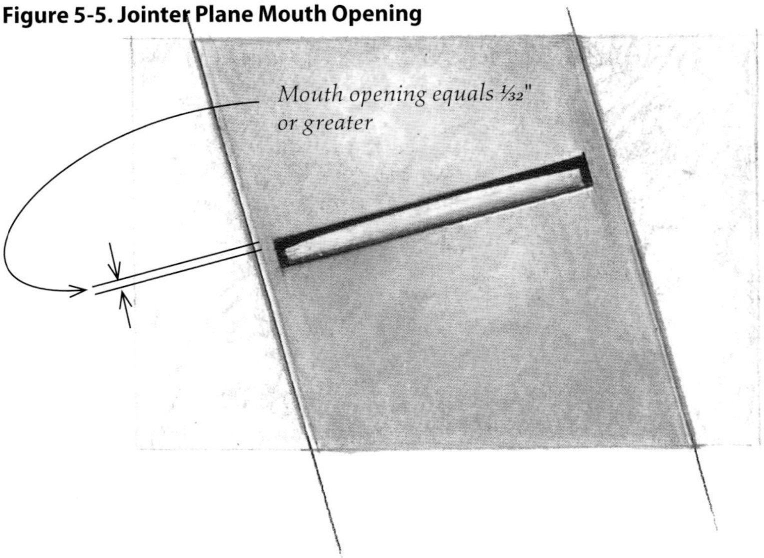

Mouth opening equals ¹⁄₃₂" or greater

The Jointer Plane

After generally straightening and roughly dimensioning the stock with the jack, the jointer (Figure 5-4)—a long, wide plane— is used to remove the roughness left by the jack and to true surfaces and edges in preparation for final smoothing. Today, the jointer plane (Figure 5-5) is most commonly about 22" (559mm) long (the Stanley #07, for example). In the past, longer planes of 24" to 30" (610mm to 762mm) often were used (such as the Stanley #08, their longest). The jointer planes long length and greater width—the blade is usually 2⅜" (60mm) to 2¾" (70mm) wide—results in a flat surface overall. Its wide blade, traditionally sharpened to a gentle curvature of about ¹⁄₃₂" (0.8mm) or less (perhaps even less if you are edge-joining very thick boards)—takes out the ridges left by the coarsely set jack, and aids in squaring

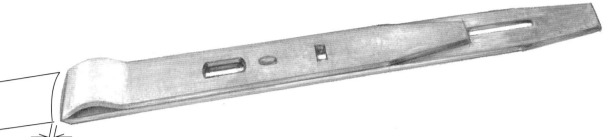

Curvature of blade

Figure 5-6. *Curvature of jointer blade: About ¹⁄₃₂" (0.8mm) over a 2¾" (70mm) width for a jointer-plane blade that is used for surfacing lumber. About ¹⁄₆₄" (0.4mm) or less on a plane used primarily for edge-jointing. Use less curvature on narrower blades and on blades set at higher cutting angles.*

THE CORRECT BLADE SHAPE

While the amount of curvature of the edge is at the discretion of the woodworker, it is important that a sweep to the edge tapers off the corners of the blade because it allows you to adjust the edge of the board being planed to square while the plane itself remains in solid contact with the work (see "Techniques for Shooting an Edge" on page 154). The edge of a jointer plane blade is not sharpened straight unless it is used with a shooting board.

board edges (Figure 5-6). The chipbreaker is set back from the blade edge the distance of the thickest shaving. Old wooden jointers typically had a cutting angle of 45° to 47½° higher than the jack, but less than the smooth plane, to reduce tearout and the effort needed to work the plane, which often makes thick shavings. The sole is trued dead flat or may be relieved slightly in strategic places to simplify keeping it true.

CAN YOU GET BY WITHOUT A JOINTER PLANE?

You probably can work without a jointer plane, but for the best quality work, only good power tools, well maintained and properly operated, will accomplish something comparable. And even then you have to evaluate the quality of the surface made by these machines. Glue-line ripping saws and well-maintained and accurate power jointers (large enough for the work) are adequate for good quality (and quantity) work. But for work we expect to outlive us, the fineness of the glued edge must be attended to. So let us look at this edge in detail.

Under a microscope, the ripped or sawn edge looks torn. Even with the best blades, there are some scoring marks, some small irregularities. Most glues bond best when the fibers are cleanly sheared, and the surfaces closely mated. A sawn surface compromises both of these qualities. However, most modern glues are gap-filling to the extent necessary between two well sawn surfaces and provide strength in excess of the wood itself; so for good quality work, sawn surfaces can be adequate if done well.

However, I believe the true longevity of this joint is in question. Edge-glued planks, such as in a tabletop, are under tremendous stress over the years and have no mechanical advantage (such as a mortise-and-tenon joint does) to resist the stresses—they depend solely on the strength of the glue. If you have ever seen a 200-year-old tabletop, you know what I mean. If the cupping of the planks has not opened the joints, then differential moisture from the seasons or central heating has opened the joints at the ends. We place a great deal of faith in our modern glues, and they appear to be miracle workers. Hide glue and the other protein glues have been around since before the time of the pharaohs, so we know pretty much how they react. However, our modern glues are only one or two generations old, and while testing assures us they are durable, the testing only mimics our best guesses and cannot possibly include all the variables. We do not actually know how they will react in the long term.

Our responsibility as woodworkers is to understand wood movement, to take into account the reaction of the wood during the gluing process as well as afterwards, and to give the glue the best conditions under which to function. We can design the piece as best we can and select the wood for optimal structural functionality (as well as grain appearance), making sure the wood is dry and has reached equilibrium with its environment. We can prepare the joint, finessing it for gluing. To do this, it tradition recommends the mating edges be planed to a slight concavity over their length, so that clamping them together produces slightly increased pressure at the ends. As the glue dries and gives off moisture at the ends of the joints first, the pressure equalizes and the joints at the ends will not open up. This finessing also increases the longevity of the joint as seasonal changes in temperature and humidity affect the open pores of the end grain first and the rest of the plank lags behind. This differential movement over the length of the plank also stresses the glue joint. The slight pressure created by planing a bit of concavity along the length of the joint helps keep the joint together. A machine cannot do this subtle shaping. It is done by skilled hands with a jointer plane, by a crafter who understands his material.

I conjecture as well that the slight concavity across the *width* of the joint resulting from the blade being sharpened to a curve contributes to the longevity of the joint. The resulting surfaces put slightly more pressure at the outside edges, combating both the initial stress from the glue drying from the outside in as well as differential movement from the outside of the board responding more quickly to seasonal changes. However, this is only a conjecture, and would be more difficult to verify than what experience over the years has shown to be true about planing a bit of curve over the length of the board.

**Figure 5-7. Bailey #4 Smoothing Plane.
Traditional Western Coffin-sided Smoother**

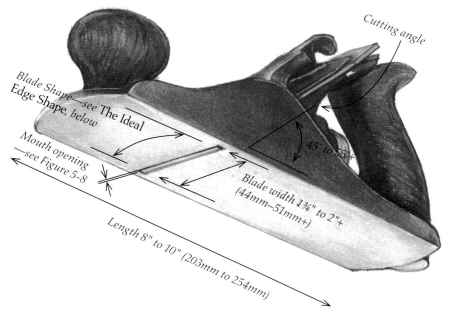

Cutting angle

*Blade Shape—see The Ideal
Edge Shape, below*

*Mouth opening
—see Figure 5-8*

45° to 55°+

*Blade width 1¾" to 2"+
(44mm–51mm+)*

Length 8" to 10" (203mm to 254mm)

THE IDEAL EDGE SHAPE

Ideally, the edge of a smoothing plane should be straight across, with the ends tapered off to avoid leaving tracks in the work. The taper needs to equal the depth of cut, which may be less than 0.005" (0.13mm). This is most easily achieved by added pressure at each corner when sharpening: five strokes for each corner on the first sharpening stone (in addition to sharpening the main edge), a few more than that on the finishing stone(s) can be enough. The resulting configuration works well, but I could not swear that it looks like the drawing.

This kind of care, precision, finesse, and craftsmanship is what sets the skilled woodworker, the conscientious studio furniture maker, apart from the manufacturer.

Smoothing Planes

With the Bailey-style planes (Figure 5-7) you can choose from the #1, #2, #3, #4, and #4½ for use as a smoothing plane. These range in length from about 5½" to 10", with blade widths from 1 ³⁄₁₆" to 2⅜". The #4 is by far the most popular and perhaps the most useful, with the #3 a close second for smaller hands and smaller work. The #1, which is quite small, and the #2 are generally used for smaller work, while the extra width on the #4½ aids in getting a flat surface. Some craftsmen will use the #5½ or #6 as an intermediate smoother for large boards and panels. The general rule is to use small planes for small work, wider planes for wider work, and longer or larger planes for longer work. The craftsman makes the choice based on his experience.

The blade sharpens either to a shallow curve not exceeding the depth of the blade set (a few thousandths of an inch) or dead straight with the corners slightly rounded off. Both techniques prevent the blade corners from digging in and leaving steps in the work, undesirable because this is the last plane to be used, and the resulting surface must be defect-free. The chipbreaker is set right down to the edge, back only as far as the thickest shaving for which the plane will be set (Figure 5-8). Blade angles can be the highest of all the planes of the triumvirate.

Ideally, the smoothing plane should be as wide as possible—as wide as or wider than the jointer. This will result in a flatter surface because though it's perhaps only a few thousandths of an inch deep, the resulting cut is basically a shallow trough. The wider it is in relation to its depth, the less perceptible it will be. There should be as well a progression in the blade widths of the planes of the triumvirate, progressing from the jack (the narrowest), to the jointer (wider), and then the smoother (the widest). However, in reality this ideal relationship of the smoothing plane to the jack and jointer is difficult to maintain when working with harder woods.

Because the cutting angle of the smoothing plane is the highest of all the planes and the blade is cutting its full width (unlike the jack, and often the jointer plane, which often are not set to make a cut the full depth of the sweep of their blade), the amount of resistance to the cut is very high. A wide blade, though making a very shallow cut, will have greater resistance than a narrow blade. On hard woods, this can mean that for all but the lightest cut, smoothing wood will be hard work. For this reason smoothing planes traditionally have blades 1¾" (44mm) to 2" (51mm) wide, even though jointers

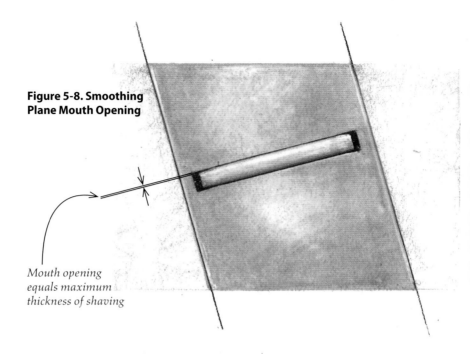

Figure 5-8. Smoothing Plane Mouth Opening

Mouth opening equals maximum thickness of shaving

traditionally are much wider than that, with blades 2⅜" (60mm) to 2¾" (70mm) wide. Because of these factors, generally, I would tend to limit blade widths on planes with cutting angles of 50° and greater to 2" (51mm) or less.

Short planes can be particularly useful in smoothing difficult woods. The converse of the functional shape of the jointer plane applies: while the length of the jointer trues a surface by bridging the hills and valleys, a very short plane will smooth the surface by following them. The best way to approach difficult woods, after leveling with a jointer, is to prepare the surface with a smoothing plane finely set to true the surface, followed by an even more finely set smoother, of shorter proportion, that follows the surface and smoothes any remaining roughness.

WHY A NARROW SMOOTHER?

Making the smoothing plane narrower than the jointer can make setting up and tuning it a little less demanding. A narrower smoother also makes accessing the entire surface of the work easier without annoying and unproductive *skips*. This is especially important with hardwoods because they can be prone to tearout and must be worked with a very finely set blade.

WHAT TO LOOK FOR IN A SMOOTHING PLANE

Blade quality is the most important consideration in selecting a smoothing plane. The other tactics of plane anatomy fall in line after this priority. It must be possible to execute these tactics finely and precisely, and, just as importantly, the settings must be easy to maintain.

A more expensive plane may get you adjustment that is more precise and more dependable maintenance of fine settings, but unless the blade is of the highest quality, and matched to the work, all of that will mean nothing. In the end though, more than any of the other planes, your choice of smoothing plane is personal. Whatever your preference, get the best blade for it that you can.

To get the most efficient and effective use of the smoothing plane, all of the strategies for effective planing must be used. While a nice piece of even-grained wood may be forgiving of sloppiness in the set-up of a plane, difficult woods can be smoothed only with planes that have been precisely set and fastidiously maintained. To effectively plane the most difficult-figured woods, the critical tolerances required of blade shape, sharpness, cutting depth, and sole flatness become difficult to perceive. Maintaining the proper balance between the position of the chipbreaker and throat opening in relation to the blade angle is also difficult. However, with practice, you can begin to sense the correct tolerances or what is out of balance in the interplay between particular tactics. This *sense* bears on what we call skill, achieved only by striving for excellence through practice. Knowing and understanding the tactics is the first step. The next, more difficult, step is to know (and be able to perceive) the tolerances involved. That can only be learned through practice.

The smoothing plane is the most commonly available plane today, and perhaps the most useful. Whereas machines have largely supplanted the plane in dimensioning and truing lumber, the effectiveness of the smoothing plane is hard to cast aside. For some tasks, it is demonstrably faster, more accurate, and more effective than abrasives in producing the highest quality surface. Its main drawback is that it takes skill and practice to achieve proficiency, and skill and practice require an investment of time and training.

6

Choosing Your
First Planes

A Guide to a Suitable Toolkit

I often ruminate: If I were starting out now from scratch, what would I choose for my first plane? My second? How would I build an effective set of planes that would serve my style of working? Students have asked the question and I have tossed it around for a long time. I certainly do not have the definitive answer, but I can give my opinions and the reasons for them, and you can decide for yourself. If you end up with a plane you just never use, well, there is always a woodworker somewhere who can probably use it.

Low angle bevel-up bench planes are more versatile than their bevel-down cousins, and can be a good choice for a multi-task plane. Shown here are the Veritas Bevel-up Smoother, and on the right, their Bevel-up Jack Plane.

The number and types of planes you will eventually need depends upon the type of work you do. If you do a variety of projects, you will end up needing a variety of planes. If your range of work is narrow, you can probably get by with just a few select planes.

Buy planes—and tools in general—only as you need them. Be reluctant to buy sets unless you are sure you will be able to use all of the pieces in the set.

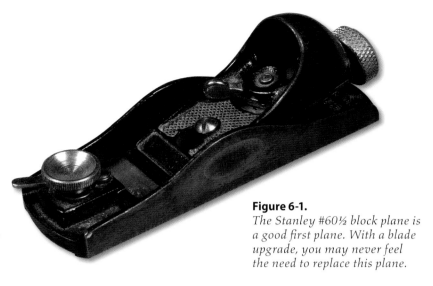

Figure 6-1.
The Stanley #60½ block plane is a good first plane. With a blade upgrade, you may never feel the need to replace this plane.

First Things First

If you are just starting out, I would recommend getting a Stanley block plane, such as the #60½, new or vintage (Figure 6-1). The Lie-Nielsen and the Veritas (now only slightly cheaper than the Lie-Nielsen), are excellent tools, but because of their price, I hesitate to suggest them as a first plane. I might look forward to upgrading to it later (Figure 6-2). Make sure the block plane you choose has an adjustable mouth and the low (12° to 13.5°) blade angle. These planes are versatile and readily accessible to the

beginner, at the same time providing good service to the more demanding, experienced professional.

A good block plane will teach you a lot about the dynamics of planing and how the different strategies work and interact. It is forgiving of mistreatment (except being dropped) and its small blade is easy to re-sharpen or grind if need be. Open the block plane's adjustable mouth and use it to remove a lot of wood for shaping. Close the mouth and it polishes difficult, figured woods. The low blade angle allows easy variations in

Figure 6-2. *These upmarket block planes, the Veritas and the even more expensive Lie-Nielsen, can be the next step up from the Stanley #60½: better blades, more precise machining, and adjustability.*

cutting angle (by honing or re-grinding the bevel angle). You can use the block plane on a bench hook or to start a chamfer without scoring the bottom of the plane (a task that cuts a V-groove on a wood-plane sole).

I prefer the low-angle #60½. I feel the low (12°) angle is inherently more versatile, as with a 25° bevel angle you get a 37° cutting angle. The lowest cutting angle you will get with the #09½, with its 20° bedding angle and a 25° bevel angle, is 45°. If you find yourself working with many difficult or tropical hardwoods, though, you might want to get the #09½ instead of, or in addition to, the #60½.

Some woodworkers will never have need for another plane, though I think once you experience the full effectiveness of this plane, you will begin to see where planes of other sizes and configurations can advance your work.

Do not get a block plane without an adjustable throat. Many of the cheapest—and, conversely, the most expensive—versions of this plane come without an adjustable throat. It would be pointless, as an adjustable throat is what gives this plane its great versatility. With it, you can have both the power stroke of a heavy farm tractor and the finesse of a fine sports car. Without it, you have just one or the other.

With the mass-market planes such as Record or Stanley, I would seriously consider upgrading the blade to a good quality alloy or laminated blade—an alloy blade if the majority of your work is shaping (mine usually is), a laminated blade if you are doing more smoothing. I have had good luck with all the laminated blades I have tried and can highly recommend the good quality ones, even for rough work. On the other hand, I have a Veritas block plane now, which came with an A2 blade. This has proven to be durable and performs well even when smoothing gnarly woods. The blade that comes with the Stanley (the only other one I have direct experience with) is good if you plan to be planing around nails and will have to regrind frequently. However, as always, let your experience and skill dictate. If the blade you have is performing satisfactorily, do not change it. If, however, you find the blade dulling quicker than you like, or you are unable, despite tuning, to get the results of which you believe the plane is capable, then upgrade the blade.

YOUR SECOND PLANE

Your next plane? There are probably a number of choices here. (I can practically see the wheels spinning in the heads of the experienced woodworkers). Knowing what I know now, and having planes available now that were not available even a short time ago, I would suggest the Veritas low-angle jack plane (based on the Stanley #62) or its

Figure 6-3. *The Lie Nielsen and (above) the Veritas low-angle jack are versatile planes suitable for many of the tasks around the shop.*

Figure 6-4.
Refurbishing an old plane like this Bailey-style #05 jack made by Millers Falls, above, can be a viable alternative to purchasing a new plane.

ADJUSTABLE THROAT PLATES

The adjustable throat plate on the Veritas does not project in front of the plane where it is vulnerable to being banged and possibly pushed back into the blade. Nevertheless, I have managed to bang it on things and push it back into the blade. I do not remember this happening with my Stanley and I think it is because the cam lever on the Stanley that adjusts the throat plate back and forth also prevents the throat plate from accidentally moving when banged. The lever also makes it easier to adjust the plate. Other than this, I think the Veritas is a far better plane and good value.

Lie-Nielsen counterpart (Figure 6-3). The jack plane has all of the features of the block plane—adjustable mouth, low-angle blade— but in a bigger size making it more efficient in planing larger surfaces. Though without the experience acquired in the set-up and use of the block plane, the jack plane could be frustrating for someone just starting out. I do not think I would make the jack plane my first plane.

With the addition of a couple of extra blades, it could be used as:

• a jack for rough-shaping surfaces (using a blade ground and sharpened to a suitable curve);

• smooth planing or panel planing (using a blade shaped with the corners honed back);

• shooting on the shooting board, or miscellaneous other precise tasks (with the blade honed straight).

Additionally, you can have blades ground to different bevel angles for planing, for instance, tropical hardwoods. (Veritas now sells blades for its version of this plane pre-ground to different bevels). The downside to this is that, as discussed in Chapter 3, this can make the bevel angle pretty blunt, thus increasing the amount of effort required to push the plane, possibly reducing the quality of the cut (depends on the wood), and usually dulling the blade quicker. This is a cheaper solution, however, than buying or making a new plane (though if I found myself doing this a lot, I would probably consider getting a dedicated plane).

Alternatively, I would consider getting a Bailey #5 jack plane (Figure 6-4). However, having a blade with the bevel down means that changing the cutting angle is not possible unless you grind a back bevel on the top of the edge. Moving the frog forward to close the mouth down is slower and more cumbersome than adjusting the mouth on the low-angle planes. On Bedrock-type models moving the frog forward changes the depth setting of the blade. (On my block plane, I readjust the mouth opening repeatedly during the day, so this adjustment needs to be quick and easy.) The chipbreaker on the #5 requires disassembly for adjustment, so it is also not an option for frequent readjustment.

Lee Valley's new line of customizable planes overcomes some of these shortcomings by using an adjustable throat plate instead of the frog to adjust the mouth opening and by having available frogs of different bedding angles. This might make it nearly as fast to readjust as the low-angle plane, and perhaps maybe more versatile in the long run because having an appropriate cutting angle matched with the correct bevel angle will give better results. However, these planes are considerably more expensive, and in addition you may need to get separate blade and chipbreaker assemblies for different frog angles: at the higher pitches the blade bevel and chipbreaker bevel may need to be altered to maintain performance and to keep the plane from jamming.

You could consider getting the short version (9" to 10") of the Low Angle Smoothing Plane, but I do not believe it is quite as versatile as the longer jack, which, because of its length, will produce surfaces

that are more accurate; and it can be used to shoot, or otherwise prepare edges for gluing, or for general smoothing of surfaces.

SMOOTHING IS NEXT

After these planes, I think the woodworker should consider getting a plane dedicated primarily to smoothing, since one of the most common tasks today is removing marks from machining and preparing pieces for finishing. You should consider a Bailey #4-size plane.

The problem is the variety of quality in this style of plane, especially with vintage planes, it takes some experience to tell which ones are going to work well, even though they all look pretty much the same. The instructions in Chapter 7 on setting up planes should help you avoid many problems. Lie-Nielsen and Clifton each make a beautiful version, which works well pretty much out of the box, but I hesitate to recommend them if you are just starting out, because of the price. Lee Valley, Woodriver, and Stanley Sweetheart make planes that are slightly cheaper though still a considerable investment for someone starting out.

It would be better to learn to set up and maintain on a cheaper plane; otherwise, after a few years of experience you will look at that plane and believe you have to apologize to it for all you put it through. As your skills increase and you look back on those first planes, you will realize how much damage you did to them learning how to set them up, tune, and maintain them. For that reason, I suggest not starting out with a $500 plane. Get a solid-quality tool suited to your skill level—one you can learn on and make mistakes with. You can upgrade as your skills progress.

When I was first starting out, I would purchase a plane for smoothing and set it up as best I could. My skills and understanding progressed over time, and I would realize my setup was not adequate for the level of performance I now required and expected. Perhaps the quality of the plane, but definitely what I did to it to set it up, was going to limit the performance of that plane. I would therefore upgrade, turning that previous plane into a preparatory plane or panel plane, and use the new plane for fine smoothing.

Beyond the Basics

After this stage, you should acquire (or make) planes as needed for specific projects, especially if you expect to do something again in that wood or on that scale.

If you do a lot of handplaning, you will find it faster to use more than one plane for smoothing. Surfaces straight from the jointer plane or the power planer can have many surface irregularities. The jointer plane, with its scalloped cut, leaves a slightly textured surface. Lumber from the power planer often will be surprisingly uneven, usually with some snipe at the ends from before and after it leaves the bed rollers, and often other irregularities, or tearout. When working the surface with a finely set and maintained smoothing plane, irregularities show up as the plane skips over them initially, leaving large areas untouched. Your first reaction is

to set the plane deeper, to avoid wasting effort cutting air. This may necessitate setting the blade deeper and, depending on the plane, opening the mouth a little and possibly backing off the chipbreaker.

If you have a screwed-on chipbreaker, you will have to disassemble the plane before you can readjust. In addition, on a surface prone to tearout, you will have to use all of the usual planing strategies to get good results. Once you have the surface leveled, you will have to close the mouth down and reset the chipbreaker and blade. If the surface is particularly difficult, the blade should be fresh from the sharpening stone. If you have already used the blade to prepare the board, you will probably need to re-sharpen it. Getting the proper setting for a fine tearout-free cut takes a bit of finessing, so adjusting it back and forth from one type of cut to another takes additional time.

To avoid adjusting, readjusting, and re-sharpening it is faster to use two and sometimes three planes for smoothing. When preparing parts for a project, I often work through the majority of the pieces with only one plane, experiencing no problems, especially when some of the surfaces are hidden. Prominent surfaces, or ones prone to tearout, may require more care. For these, after smoothing away the milling marks with the first plane, I go over the surfaces with a second, more finely set plane. Sometimes on tougher surfaces, I resort to a third plane. Each plane in the sequence has an increasingly finer set of the blade, as well as chipbreaker and throat settings, and the blades themselves are of increasing quality. The last plane I use has my best blade and is so finely set that it cuts only dead flat surfaces. This plane cuts an extremely fine slice, with shavings like gossamer, leaving a tearout-free surface. However, if the work is not prepared to a sufficient tolerance of flat, it just skips over the low spots.

Initially I used another smoothing plane the same size as the final smoother, such as a #4, for this preliminary plane—and often still do—and this works well. However, I found that using a plane larger than my final smoothing plane is often even more effective in achieving the required flat surface. The extra length, with a sole prepared as a truing plane, really levels the surface, and the use of a wide blade (2¼" to 2⅜", or 57mm to 70mm, depending on the type and size of the wood to be planed) sharpened straight with just the corners honed off, as in a finely set-up smoother, yields a flatter surface as well. I call this larger preliminary smoothing plane a *panel plane*. This panel plane is finely set up, so that it cannot make a deep cut.

If the surface is too rough coming off the machines, I will use a more coarsely set plane

(or plane/chipbreaker set honed to a greater curvature) to initially level, and then prepare the surface with the panel plane.

The panel plane has become my workhorse. Often, it is the only plane I use. Because the sole is set up as a truing plane, I know the surface it leaves will be true. In addition, because the throat, chipbreaker, and blade are set up as a fine smoother, it can plane all but the most difficult surfaces. If I have to use a finer plane, I know the surface the panel plane leaves will be flat enough that I will not have to spend a lot of time planing off the high spots until the smoothing plane is able to cut the whole surface.

The Bailey #5½, with a 2⅜"-wide blade, is ideal for this task. The #5 with a 2"-wide blade, and the low-angle jack with a 2¼"-wide blade—which you theoretically already have—can also be used; with a separate blade/chipbreaker (or blade, in the case of the low angle) ground to a ¹⁄₁₆" curvature, it can also be used for removing stock, like a traditional jack plane. (I think the #5½ is too wide for this task, at least in hardwoods.) I frankly think the #5½ was invented to be used as a smoother, mainly on large panels (hence its name) (Figure 6-5).

In this sequence of smoothing planes I am recommending, ideally the blade angles would increase as the work progresses. However, one

Figure 6-5. The Lee Valley #5½ Large Jack Plane.

of my main complaints about the Bailey planes is that they all come with a blade angle of only 45°. For northern hardwoods, and especially tropical hardwoods, this is a very low angle, which makes it hard work to eliminate tearout. Achieving good results in hardwood is easier when the blade angle is 50° or 55° (oak responds really well to 60° and tropical hardwoods to 65°+). Until recently, the only way to have planes with these blade angles was to make them yourself out of wood, as they traditionally were. This is still a good solution, but if you prefer Bailey planes (and you have the money), you can now customize your blade angles.

In this idealized world, the scenario would go like this: For northern hardwoods, the panel plane would have a blade angle of 45° or preferably 47½°; your smoother would have a blade angle of 50° and would ideally be a #4½ with a 2⅜" blade. A second smoother for more difficult woods would be a #4 with a

2"-wide blade and a 55° blade angle.

For working softwoods, the low-angle jack and #4 smoother you bought early on can be used as the panel plane and smoother, respectively.

For working tropical hardwoods, trying to avoid further investment, you can use your #4 with the 55° blade angle for smoothing, followed by scrapers, or you can use a bevel-up plane with a higher bevel angle.

If you find yourself often working with oversize timber that doesn't fit on your power jointer, you might want to invest in a *wood* jack plane, either the English pattern (Figure 6-6) or the German horned jack. These are lighter, have less friction, and are easier on the hands for heavy work. Also useful is a scrub plane, but again I would recommend the wood version, for the same reasons.

If you are working on oversize lumber, you might also find it useful to get a #6 plane. This plane fits perfectly between the jack and the jointer when preparing large surfaces. This plane is often called a "fore plane;" it is used for preparing large surfaces as well as doing the rough straightening of edges before the jointer plane (see page 74). It's a plane most people can get along without, but it does a great job when you need it.

Not too far into your career, you will need a jointer plane. The best quality work requires edges be prepared for gluing with a jointer plane, and some pieces can be properly prepared only using this plane. If the majority of your work with this plane is shooting edges and ends, and some minor

Figure 6-6. *This English-pattern jack plane was a gift—it does not get any cheaper than that. Though it is not much to look at with a chip off the top of the tote, it has a decent cast-steel blade with a good chipbreaker, and can be put into service quickly.*

flattening, the Stanley #07 (or the #08, if you can find one) is a good plane (Figure 6-7). If frequent flattening of stock is included in your jointer's job description, you might want to consider getting a wood jointer plane for the improved ergonomics and reduced friction of its sole.

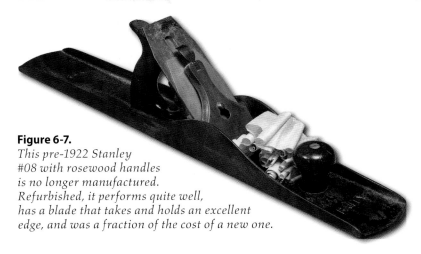

Figure 6-7.
This pre-1922 Stanley #08 with rosewood handles is no longer manufactured. Refurbished, it performs quite well, has a blade that takes and holds an excellent edge, and was a fraction of the cost of a new one.

JOINTMAKING PLANES

While it is worthwhile getting a plane for adjusting rabbets, dadoes, and other joints, I do not believe there is any need to go right out and buy one on the first day. The first time you need to adjust a joint will be soon enough (this may come the second day). I think one of the most useful tools for these kinds of adjustment is the shoulder rabbet plane. This can be used to work in dadoes to adjust the depth, smooth the machine marks left from cutting a rabbet, or taper a rabbet, adjust tenons and tenon shoulders (from whence it gets its name), and a multitude of other uses that are difficult to do any other way. The Veritas and Lie-Nielsen medium shoulder planes are good choices here, as is the Clifton, or the Clifton 3-in-1. Stanley makes a variety of rabbet planes, but so far the quality has been disappointing. I might have to give the edge to Veritas, as their plane is only $^{11}/_{16}$" (17mm) wide, which will fit into a dado cut exactly wide enough to take a piece of plywood (about $^{23}/_{64}$" or 9mm); a ¾" (19mm)-wide plane will not (Figure 6-8). Another tool that you should be aware of is the side-rabbet plane. You may be able to work around not having the side-rabbet plane your entire career in woodworking, but that

might be because you did not know it existed. Use a side-rabbet plane to widen a groove, dado, or rabbet for a nice tight fit (as opposed to not fitting at all). Nothing is as fast and accurate. You can find a vintage Stanley #79, or a #98 and #99, or buy a new version of one of these, now made by a number of manufacturers.

SUMMARY

Your basic tool kit should soon include the small block plane, low angle (bevel-up) jack, a #4 bevel-down smoother, and a shoulder rabbet plane. You may never need more planes (or maybe not even this many), but you can certainly add more as you need them and understand them.

Bottom line: Buy tools as you need them, and buy the best you can afford—and appreciate.

Figure 6-8. *The Veritas shoulder plane, doing what it was originally designed to do: trim the shoulder of a tenon.*

7

PLANE SETUP

Setting Up the Bailey/Stanley Plane

Of all the styles of planes, the ones that look the most alike but have the greatest variation in quality are the Bailey-style planes. Setting aside top-of-the-line models such as Lie-Nielsen, Clifton, Veritas, and now Woodriver, whose qualities are obvious, the remainders run the gamut. This style of plane was made by so many manufacturers—Sears, Millers Falls, Sargent, Record, Montgomery Ward—virtually every hardware franchise and big-box store. Even within the Stanley line itself, from the same period, the quality of both materials and manufacturing varied widely.

The use of a shop-made scraper speeds the conditioning of the sole of a metal plane.

When purchasing new, it is best to stay with the more respected manufacturers and avoid cheaper models. In a higher-quality plane, the milled areas for the blade and the frog will be larger and better designed, resulting in greater cutting reliability and a reduced chance of blade chatter. In addition, the adjuster will be heavier with much less slop, letting you set the blade quicker and more accurately. Buying a better version of the plane also improves your chances of getting a mature casting.

Cast iron needs to rest for about six months as it adjusts to the stresses from the casting process. Better-quality manufacturers will allow the casting to age before milling it despite the cost of allowing material inventory to sit around for six months. If they are milled before they have aged, the castings may warp out of true before they reach the end user (you)—or you have purchased, setup, and tuned it. Because of this, parts may not mate well, the cut may be unreliable, the use frustrating, and the problems difficult to correct.

Alternatively, you can purchase a vintage tool. If you choose carefully (or are just plain lucky!), with a couple hours invested in tune-up, and at worst an upgrade in a new blade and/or chipbreaker, you can have a quite serviceable tool for literally a tenth of the cost of a premium upmarket plane.

When purchasing vintage, though, name is not necessarily an indication of a worthwhile tool. In fact, when looking for a good used tool, not buying a collectible will save you money. When looking around, well-formed

handles that are fully rounded, preferably out of rosewood, will flag a plane that deserves a second look. Look to see how badly the mouth is worn; if well rounded from wear this will require a lot of work to make it crisp again. If it's deeply worn, you should probably give it a pass. Take a look at the adjuster; the fork should be well-made with little play. Pull the lever cap and look at the blade bed; it should be large, well milled and unpainted. Bonus if the sole is corrugated; generally these planes were made for the professional and not the homeowner. If this plane is undamaged, it could be a worthwhile used tool.

And just because the plane is old, do not assume it will perform better. Many planes made for casual users were not high quality. Lower-quality planes are more likely to have been misused and may be damaged in ways not readily apparent. Such planes can also have annoyingly sloppy adjusters or trouble holding their adjustment. On the other hand, if you spot an old plane that obviously has been well used, but also well maintained, you might want to give it a second look. A used but well-maintained

Figure 7-1. *A small crack a little more than ¼" (6mm) long in the upper corner of the mouth of this plane, parallel to the side, makes this plane unusable.*

plane may have performed well for its previous owner.

Setup and tuning are similar for planes of all styles and functions. Basic procedures are performed in a specific order to set the plane up, followed by tweaking of the various tactics—throat opening, blade shape, bevel angle, etc.—which will determine the plane's function. In all cases the same basic procedures are followed in the same order:

1. Inspect the plane for condition issues
2. Prepare the blade
3. Prepare and fit the chipbreaker
4. Bed the blade properly
5. Configure the sole
6. Adjust the mouth
7. Attend to the details of the body and sole
8. Attend to the details related to the grip and finish

STEP 1: INSPECT THE PLANE

When checking out a plane, first, look at the body. On all planes, the quality of the finish may give clues to what you can expect from the plane: is the plane "japanned" (a baked enamel) or just painted? Is it sloppy or well done? Is it coarsely sanded or finely finished? What are the handles made of and how well are they finished? Inspect the body of a used plane carefully for cracks, especially around the throat (Figure 7-1). You may have to try to bend or twist the plane with your hands (do not lock it in a vise and pry on it with another tool!) to get a suspected fault to open up for sure. If the body is cracked at the throat—unless it is a particularly valuable model that might be worth brazing—discard

it. Do not bother to tune it up; the crack will render it next to useless.

Examine the blade seat. On the cheapest versions of the Bailey plane, the surfaces of the blade seat (and the frog seat on the body of the plane) are not even milled, with the rough casting simply painted over. As these areas are very difficult to correct, if it appears that the frog rocks and cannot be set solidly or if these areas are badly done, painted, or not milled at all, stop here (Figure 7-2). That plane will never make a fine shaving and

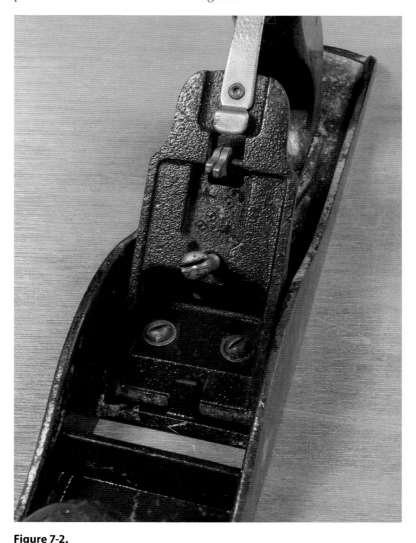

Figure 7-2.
The blade seat on a cheap plane: the bed remains unmilled and painted over.

never give more than basic utility service. Get another plane or save this one for removing paint from used boards.

On all models, check that the adjustment mechanisms will allow you the settings you may require of the plane: heavy cut, very fine cut, fine mouth setting, etc. Sometimes the adjusters run out of adjustment at the extremes. For instance, on some Bedrock-style planes, because the blade descends as the frog is moved forward, the blade depth-adjuster can run out of adjustment when the frog is moved forward to close the mouth down to a very narrow gap. This particular malady is often a result of a misplaced hole for the depth-adjuster nib on the chipbreaker. Exchanging the chipbreaker to correct this may not be an option, as many of them are specific to their own particular model and will not work in other makes or models of planes. This will limit using the tactic of closing the mouth down, which may be a liability depending on what you want to use your plane for. Also, on an old plane, sometimes the chipbreaker has been exchanged and as a result, will not give a satisfactory range of adjustment. This can be remedied by replacing it with the correct chipbreaker for that model—assuming, of course, that it was manufactured correctly the first time.

Check the operation of the blade (depth) and lateral adjusters. See that they operate freely and are not distorted, bent, or broken,

and engage the blade and chipbreaker fully. Some woodworkers have suggested that twisting the fork that engages the wheel of the blade adjuster will decrease the play in the adjustment mechanism. I have not had success doing this, and in some models, it is not possible anyway, as the fork is cast.

If you get a real flea-market find, you should take it totally apart and clean it, especially if there's any rust. This will also let you check more thoroughly for cracks and damage. Carefully unscrew all the screws; if they seem to be frozen, do not force them. Spray their base with some WD-40 and let it soak until they can be loosened without danger of breaking. Clean crud and dirt off with a brass or stainless steel brush; clean mating parts with red Scotch-Brite until they are totally clean. Brush screw threads off and put a drop of oil into their hole. You can clean and buff more, and even re-enamel, but that's not necessary to get a functioning plane.

STEP 2: PREPARE THE BLADE

A new blade, or an old blade that needs to be rejuvenated, is always prepared by flattening the back first. If there are serious nicks in the blade, the bevel may be ground first to remove them, and then the back prepared. After the back has been flattened to a mirror polish, then the bevel is honed. Although honing involves alternately stoning both the bevel and the back to remove the wire edge

FLATTENING THE BACK OF A PLANE BLADE

There are a number of techniques that can be used to flatten the back of a plane blade. Which technique to best choose in flattening a particular blade is dependent upon how much work must be done to get it flat.

No matter which technique you use, you will have to finish with your sharpening stones, and these must be flat, so start by flattening your sharpening stones. (See "Using and Maintaining Waterstones" on page 139.)

Before starting work on the blade, appraise the flatness of the back. Hold the blade up to a large light source, sighting along the blade so that you can catch a reflection that goes all the way across the back. Tilt the length of the blade up and down and study the reflection. If the entire back lights up down to the edge, you have a dead flat blade and you will only have to hone it through your usual series of stones. If, however, only a portion of the length of the blade lights up and this moves up and down the blade as you tilt it, then the blade has a curve to it: the shorter the reflection the more the curve.

In this case, do not try to flatten the entire length of the blade. (In this case, *the entire length of the blade* is from the edge up to about ¼" (6mm) away from the chipbreaker screw slot.) Only the lower portion—about ½" (13mm) minimum to maybe 1" (25mm)—needs to be flattened, depending on your blade's curve. Flattening more is incredibly tedious, requiring the removal of a lot of steel. More importantly, it is not necessary to get a functioning blade.

Finally, look at the back edge. Tilt the blade until the reflection rolls down to the edge. If you have to tilt the blade more than a little to catch a reflection there, or if you can continue tilting the blade and continue getting a reflection, indicating a rounded edge, then a different strategy is called for. In this case, before starting to flatten the back, you should grind the main blade bevel back until the rounding or back bevel is eliminated.

After you have appraised the condition of the back of your blade, developed a strategy, and made sure your stones are flat, begin flattening by stroking the blade's back on your coarsest stone. Hold the blade perpendicular to the length of the stone, use the entire length of the stone, and as much of the full width as possible, back and forth, keeping at least 1" (25mm) or more of the blade on the stone at all times.

Make sure the blade stays flat on the stone—no lifting or rocking. Keep pressure on the blade right behind the edge to keep from gouging the back. After about 30 seconds to a minute, clean and look at the back of the blade. If the new flat is within about 1/32" (0.8mm) of the edge at all places (check the reflection as before), you can probably continue using the waterstones for the whole process, moving to each individual stone as the polish pattern of each becomes continuous across and down to the entire edge.

If you have to spend more than about four or five minutes of continuous work on a waterstone, you will have to re-flatten it before continuing. Therefore, if a minute of vigorous work on the coarse stone leaves more than about 1/32" (0.8mm) of edge undone, you are probably better off going instead to a coarse diamond stone to flatten the blade. If not, you can wear your waterstones out of flat, necessitating re-flattening the stones (and most probably the back) several times before you are done. (If you have ceramic or Arkansas stones you can probably do the whole flattening process on either of those. Just make sure they're flat before you start and remain flat as you work as they do wear, albeit much more slowly.) After the flat on the back reaches the edge, you can go back and do your normal sharpening sequence on your (flat) stones to polish the back.

If after about a minute on your coarse stone you show the new flat at 1/16" (2mm) or more away, consider measures that are more drastic (though you can continue to work away on the diamond stone if you prefer). The cheapest, fastest, and most effective way to flatten a badly out-of-flat plane-blade back is to use the Japanese method of carborundum (silicon-carbide) on an iron plate *(kanaban)*. The carborundum particles grip the softer kanaban (though it does wear it out—eventually), and abrades the tool steel. The iron flattening plate, at tool suppliers, is about $25. An ounce of carborundum is about $3, though if you can find a lapidary supply house you can get a lifetime supply for about $5.

The beauty of this method is that the grit breaks down as you use it, so you can start with 60 or 90 grit, which is very coarse (for a blade in particularly bad condition), or 120 grit (if you think the blade is not too bad). Either gradually breaks down to about 6,000 grit, while increasingly refining the surface. In one step (and about 5 to

FLATTENING THE BACK OF A PLANE BLADE *(continued)*

10 minutes of vigorous rubbing), you can go from a nasty old blade to a mirror-polished jewel.

To use the flattening plate, put about ¼ teaspoon of carborundum in the center of the plate and add 3 or 4 drops of water to it **(Figure 1)**. Begin rubbing the back of

Figure 1. *To flatten a severely out-of-flat blade on a kanaban (iron plate), put about ¼ teaspoon of carborundum in the center of the plate. Add 3 or 4 drops of water to the carborundum. In the background is a stick that can be used when holding the blade.*

Figure 2. *Rub the back of the blade back and forth using the whole length of the plate. Use of a stick allows you to increase the pressure on the blade at its edge while reducing finger fatigue. The blade and stick are held with the right hand, with the left hand keeping a constant downward pressure. Do not be tempted to rock the blade. The blade must remain flat on the stone at all times. If you lift the right hand even one stroke you will round the edge enough to require 15 or 10 strokes to remove the damage.*

the blade back and forth using the whole length of the plate. Periodically bring the excess carborundum back into the center of the plate so all the carborundum is broken down at the same rate **(Figure 2)**. Stray coarse pieces of carborundum will scratch the blade, so make sure it is all used. Continue rubbing as the carborundum breaks down into a smooth paste, occasionally adding a drop or two of water if the paste gets too dry to rub. As the paste gets extremely fine, check your progress; you should see a consistent flat at the edge.

Continue rubbing until the back shows a high polish and the paste is transparently fine and rubbed dry **(Figure 3)**. Then add 1 (or maybe 2) drops of water and vigorously rub until the paste is dry again. This will bring up a very high polish. Inspect the blade. Hopefully, the mirror polish of your newly flat back now extends all the way to the edge. If not, you will have to do it again, though you can probably start with 120 or 220 grit now. With the final polish, you do not have to follow up with any work on the stones; you can go right to the bevel.

Make sure to keep the carborundum separate from your stones, because it can embed itself and continue to scratch a blade for a long time. Wash the blade and everything else in separate water and rinse thoroughly.

Figure 3. *The carborundum has broken down into a paste and is rubbed until dry.*

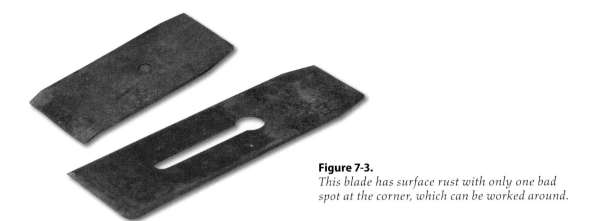

Figure 7-3.
This blade has surface rust with only one bad spot at the corner, which can be worked around.

once the back has been polished, sharpening involves only touching up the back on the final polishing stone and not reworking it with all the stones used when first flattening it.

Before starting, remove the chipbreaker and inspect the edge of the blade for damage and the back for rust severe enough to cause pitting that is too deep to be honed out (Figure 7-3). Such pits, when the edge is sharpened down to them, will leave a track in the finish work. If the blade is to be used on a relatively rough plane, a jack plane for instance, some minor pitting might be allowed, as the planes to follow will erase any tracks left behind. However, the blade will overheat in the area of these pits, rapidly dulling the blade and necessitating frequent re-sharpening or even regrinding.

After inspecting the blade, grind the bevel if necessary to remove any nicks and/or to shape the edge. Flatten the back down to a mirror polish, then go back, and sharpen the edge. (See Chapter 8, "Sharpening Plane Blades.")

STEP 3: PREPARE THE CHIPBREAKER

As indicated in "Chipbreaker" on page 42, though they all function the same, chipbreakers take several forms. Despite the slight variations, the procedures for preparing them are similar.

Inspect the chipbreaker for a damaged or badly formed edge. If the problem is severe, see if you will have enough metal left after removing the damage to have a functioning chipbreaker; if not, replace it. Refine the shape of the top contour so there is a microbevel that meets the blade at an angle of about 50°, or such an angle that the combination of blade angle and chipbreaker angle totals 90° to 100°. If the particular configuration allows enough material to

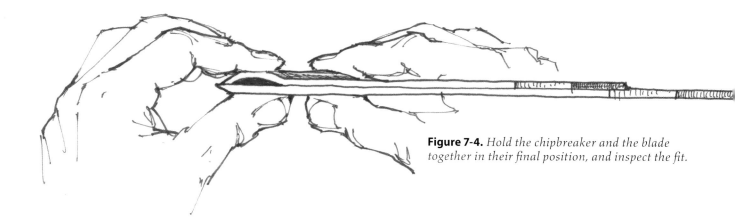

Figure 7-4. *Hold the chipbreaker and the blade together in their final position, and inspect the fit.*

remain, put a large second bevel of about 25° behind the microbevel. (You will not be able to do this on a Stanley-type chipbreaker.) The second bevel improves chip clearance and helps eliminate throat clogging. Some of the after-market chipbreakers come with this configuration.

Next, hold the chipbreaker and the blade together in their final position, and then up to a light (Figure 7-4). No light should appear between the edge of the chipbreaker and the back of the blade. Correct the edge of the chipbreaker if necessary, maintaining its geometry, by stoning the underside on a perfectly flat stone (Figure 7-5). If the edge is badly off, careful work with a smooth file may speed this step, followed by careful stoning. Back-bevel the underside of the chipbreaker slightly so that it meets the blade at a knife's edge (Figure 7-6).

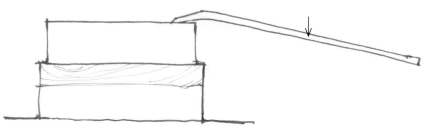

Figure 7-5. *Position the chipbreaker on the stone slightly below horizontal to ensure the edge is slightly back-beveled.*

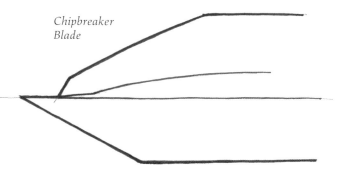

Chipbreaker
Blade

Figure 7-6. *Undercut a degree or so to ensure contact at front edge.*

Both the underside and the top microbevel closest to the edge should be stoned down to a polish (Figure 7-7). Finish the last strokes of the stoning on the top to ensure that the edge will meet tightly to the blade (Figure 7-8). Hold the chipbreaker and blade up to the light again (Figure 7-4) and check the fit. If the edge appears straight, but is high on one corner and squeezing them together does not close the gap, twist the chipbreaker to straighten it, so the edge fully contacts the blade and no light shows. Make sure that the chipbreaker is sprung slightly so that tightening its screw attachment brings the edge of the chipbreaker down tight to the blade (Figure 7-9). In some cases, the chipbreaker may have to be bent slightly to achieve this.

WORKING AROUND THE BLADE-ADJUSTMENT NIB

Because the blade-adjustment nib protrudes above the blade bed, is pinned, and cannot be removed, any overall flattening of the bed will have to be done piecemeal working around the nib. Working like this will most likely make its condition worse. Leave it alone. Just look for protrusions of enamel or missed milling. If the overall flatness of the bed is bad—get another plane.

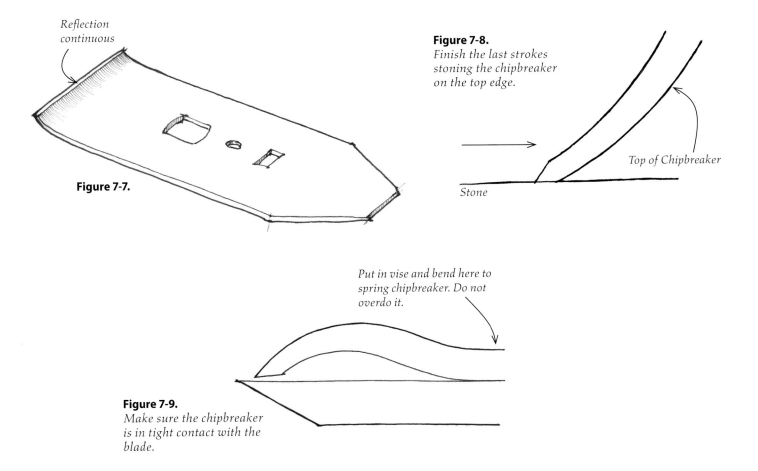

Reflection continuous

Figure 7-7.

Figure 7-8.
Finish the last strokes stoning the chipbreaker on the top edge.

Top of Chipbreaker

Stone

Put in vise and bend here to spring chipbreaker. Do not overdo it.

Figure 7-9.
Make sure the chipbreaker is in tight contact with the blade.

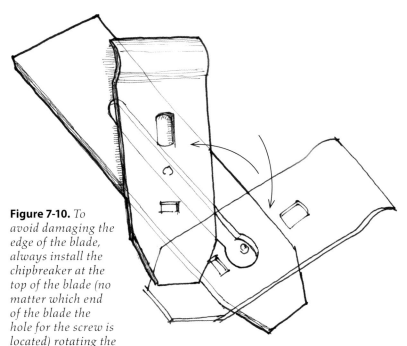

Figure 7-10. *To avoid damaging the edge of the blade, always install the chipbreaker at the top of the blade (no matter which end of the blade the hole for the screw is located) rotating the chipbreaker over the blade and down into position.*

dirt under either one can cause the blade to chatter.

Inspect the frog and plane's mating surfaces for the same problems, and correct minor aberrations with a file or diamond file as before. With the screws replaced but left slightly loose, see if it can be rocked on its mating surfaces. Experiment with the screws lightly tightened to verify the frog

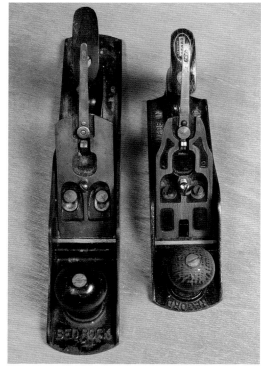

Attach the chipbreaker to the blade (Figure 7-10), adjust its position according to the work to be done, check again, finally, that no light comes through the meeting of the two at the edge, and tighten the screw down

STEP 4: BED THE BLADE PROPERLY

On a decent-quality plane, all of the surfaces of the blade seat and the back edge of the mouth opening will be nicely milled and free of enamel, needing at most only cleanup of a little bit of enamel or a recalcitrant corner or a bit of flash missed by the milling machine (Figure 7-11). Clean it up carefully with a file. Remove the two screws residing under the blade that attach the frog to the body of the plane, and remove the frog. (Be certain the frog-adjustment screws do not protrude above the level of the bed when fully tightened and interfere with the bedding of the blade.) Make sure the blade bed and the frog's mating surfaces are clean; a little bit of

Figure 7-11. *The older plane (above left in Figure 7-11) has a considerably larger contact area on the blade bed, though it is not clear whether this makes any real difference in the performance of the plane. The contact area for the frog in each plane (below) is about the same.*

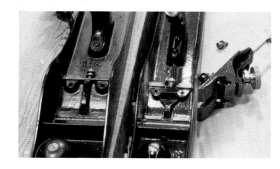

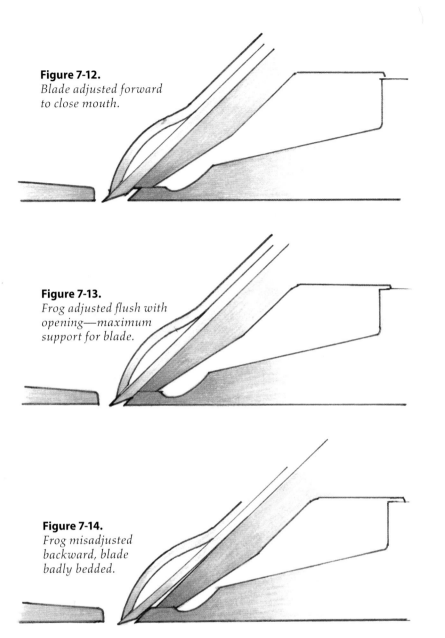

Figure 7-12.
Blade adjusted forward to close mouth.

Figure 7-13.
Frog adjusted flush with opening—maximum support for blade.

Figure 7-14.
Frog misadjusted backward, blade badly bedded.

it, you can use the "tapping" technique to discover the mating surface that is not making contact. Do this by holding down the frog tightly in the center with only one finger. Take a finger of the opposite hand and tap each of the four corners in turn. The corner that makes a tapping sound when struck is not making contact. Working on the frog and not the main body, take a little metal off the mating surface adjacent to it (on the same level) until the tapping sound stops. Hopefully, the frog remains workably square and parallel to everything when you're done, and you've not made it worse.

Reinstall the frog and check that the opening of the mouth at the back (frog side) is square to the length of the plane, and that the frog can be made parallel to it.

The frog and the back of the throat at the body form the seat of the blade (unless you have a Bedrock-type plane, in which case the blade is completely supported by the frog) and the two must be able to form a continuous flat plane (Figures 7-12, 7-13, and 7-14). Hopefully, the frog can be set back far enough and rotated if necessary to align with this edge. A little bit of filing on the edge of the back of the mouth might be called for if the frog cannot be rotated enough. I would recommend not filing, though, because it can bring about a cascade of problems, and blade adjustment will compensate (within limits) for out of square anyway.

Unless you are doing some exceptionally fine planing, adjust the frog to give the blade its maximum support: that is, aligned with

can be securely and solidly bedded. If it can't, this is very difficult to correct. I'm tempted to say that, unless this is an otherwise particularly good plane or one of sentimental value, you should get another plane. If this is a new plane, definitely take it back. The mating surfaces are difficult to access with a file, particularly when you are trying to keep things parallel and flat. Though I don't recommend it, if you want to try and correct the back edge of the mouth of the body. Insert the blade, making sure it is properly seated, the hole in the chipbreaker over the blade-adjuster nib, and the slot in the blade over the nib of the lateral-adjustment knob. Adjust the lever cap's screw so that there is only enough pressure to keep the blade from shifting around under its workload. Too much pressure, and there is danger of damaging the plane.

STEP 5: CONFIGURE THE SOLE

(Note: I strongly suggest you reread "Length of Plane/Width of Blade" on page 52. On new, top-of-the-line planes you should have to do little, if any, truing of the sole. I would, in fact, seriously consider returning it if I had to do any. If, over time, the sole becomes worn (they do wear!), especially at the mouth, or the cast iron moves, you can then touch it up as described.)

The basic concept for flattening and configuring the sole of a plane is that all we need is a minimum of three parallel contact areas, the width of the sole, all on a line; areas in between these are relieved *slightly* ($\pm 0.002"$) to reduce maintenance. There are always at least two in front of the cutting edge: one at the very front and one right at the mouth of the plane, and they form the basic reference area for moving the plane over the work. And there is always at least one behind the blade, its location dependent on the task the plane is expected to do—dimension, true, or smooth.

Based on practical experience and the traditional practice of Japanese woodworkers, I suggest a further refinement. On some planes, relieve the contact area(s) behind the blade a small amount instead of keeping it in the same plane as the two (or more) areas in front of the blade. The actual amount depends on the task the plane is expected to do. My suggestion is for planes used for truing a surface, such as jointers, to have all their contact surfaces all in the same line. Smoothing planes should have the contact area behind the blade relieved ever so slightly to facilitate the plane reaching into any very slight low areas of the work that might remain from previous preparation. And on longer planes, especially truing planes, there are more than three contact planes.

Jack planes could, at your discretion, have the reference area behind the blade relieved slightly more than what the smoothing plane is relieved to make it easier to attack areas when initially dimensioning a piece. Configuring the sole like this, besides facilitating maintenance and the task the plane is expected to do, also helps deal with the continued distortion of the sole that results from the blade-fixing action of the lever cap tending to push the sole down. This stress is dynamic and changes easily. In order to deal with this variable, I do not have any contact areas right here in my planes, but further back beyond the blade bed area (Figure 7-15).

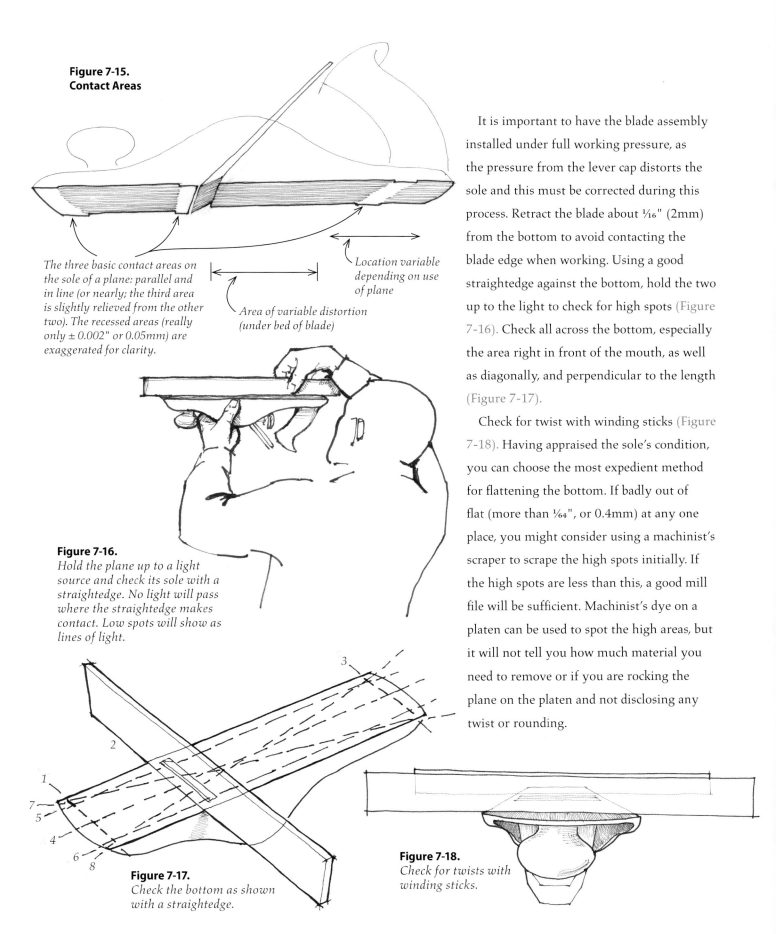

**Figure 7-15.
Contact Areas**

The three basic contact areas on the sole of a plane: parallel and in line (or nearly; the third area is slightly relieved from the other two). The recessed areas (really only ± 0.002" or 0.05mm) are exaggerated for clarity.

Area of variable distortion (under bed of blade)

Location variable depending on use of plane

Figure 7-16.
Hold the plane up to a light source and check its sole with a straightedge. No light will pass where the straightedge makes contact. Low spots will show as lines of light.

Figure 7-17.
Check the bottom as shown with a straightedge.

Figure 7-18.
Check for twists with winding sticks.

It is important to have the blade assembly installed under full working pressure, as the pressure from the lever cap distorts the sole and this must be corrected during this process. Retract the blade about $\frac{1}{16}$" (2mm) from the bottom to avoid contacting the blade edge when working. Using a good straightedge against the bottom, hold the two up to the light to check for high spots (Figure 7-16). Check all across the bottom, especially the area right in front of the mouth, as well as diagonally, and perpendicular to the length (Figure 7-17).

Check for twist with winding sticks (Figure 7-18). Having appraised the sole's condition, you can choose the most expedient method for flattening the bottom. If badly out of flat (more than $\frac{1}{64}$", or 0.4mm) at any one place, you might consider using a machinist's scraper to scrape the high spots initially. If the high spots are less than this, a good mill file will be sufficient. Machinist's dye on a platen can be used to spot the high areas, but it will not tell you how much material you need to remove or if you are rocking the plane on the platen and not disclosing any twist or rounding.

GENERAL TECHNIQUES FOR ADJUSTING THE PLANE BLADE

Adjust the blade by turning the plane over and sighting down the sole from the front of the plane **(Figure 1)**. Hold the plane so that the background or lighting provides contrast between the black line of the blade protruding and the light reflecting off the sole. Using the plane's adjustment mechanism, advance the blade until you can just see it begin to protrude below the sole as a thin black line. Adjust the blade laterally until this line is parallel to the sole. Advance or retreat according to your best guess of the depth of shaving you want. Make a trial and re-adjust as necessary.

Needless to say, sometimes the blade can be hard to see, especially if it is set fine, you are a beginner, or you have aging eyes—or all three. Sometimes you find the black line you thought was the blade was actually the bed of the blade—and you wondered why the blade stubbornly refused to cut. Sometimes on a steeply pitched blade, there is too little contrast between the blade and the sole of the plane. In this case, you are better off sighting down the sole from the back where the light will shine off the bevel of the blade and contrast with the mouth opening.

Another technique some woodworkers recommend, and one I use to supplement the others, is lightly feeling the protrusion of the corners of the blade with your thumbs **(Figure 2)**. This would seem to risk cutting your thumbs, but the technique is quite common, and I have seen both Westerners and Japanese craftsmen use it. It is a good way to tell if the corners of the blade are protruding evenly, though I have yet to get the hang of using this technique to the exclusion of the others.

Figure 1. *Sight down the sole of the plane to see the depth the blade is set at.*

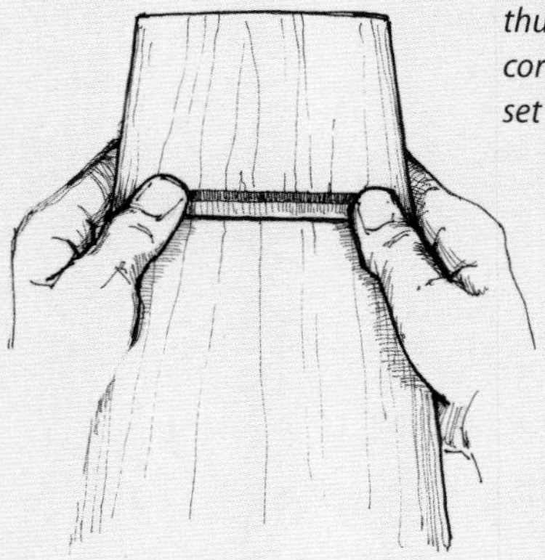

Figure 2. *Use your thumbs to check that the corners of the blade are set equally.*

WHAT REALLY HAPPENS

If you examined what happens when a plane cuts, it might appear the area behind the blade should be exactly in line with the blade edge and project more than the two areas in front—much like how the outfeed table of a power jointer is set up—nearly even with the cutters.

In practice, however, it is often helpful to slightly relieve the third working surface, not only from the blade edge, but often from the other two leading surfaces as well. This is because as the blade edge wears, it withdraws—gets shorter (see "How an Edge Dulls" on page 51)—and a plane bottom that was fixed even with the sharpened edge would soon hold the worn edge off the work.

I do not recommend you do all the leveling with sandpaper, especially if you have a lot to do. I have found a lot of sanding results in a distorted bottom rather than a flat one. I think the distortion results from the slight repetitive error in weight shift that happens over hundreds of strokes. If you have had some experience in sharpening, you know you can take more material off one part of the blade simply by putting more pressure on that area. I have found that this happens when using sandpaper to flatten the sole of a plane. In order to reduce the time tediously grinding away at the sole on sandpaper and actually inducing error rather than correcting it, I recommend, after checking the sole and becoming familiar with its terrain, that you relieve the high spots with faster techniques such as a machinist's scraper and/or files. It is better to carefully remove material indicated by a straightedge, and/or

machinist's bluing (or the scratch pattern of sandpaper on a flat surface) with a file and to reserve the sandpaper for polishing out the file marks and bringing the contact areas into perfect alignment (Figure 7-19). Doing it this way results in much less material the sandpaper has to remove, increased accuracy, and reduced time spent. In fact, after filing, if sanding does not level the sole to the degree required after about three minutes,

Figure 7-19. *The scratch pattern after about one minute rubbing on sandpaper on a granite platen. The bright areas have been sanded. Notice the darker area, in front of the mouth; this area is slightly lower and has not been sanded. This critical area needs to be brought into line. The dark oval top center is a depression resulting from distortion of the casting because of the extra thickness at the handle mount. This area can remain depressed, so long as a flat toward the back of the plane is established.*

you should go back to filing before returning to sanding. Sanding for more than three minutes before checking could distort the bottom.

The entire sole of your plane does not have to be dead flat (unless maybe you're a pattern maker); it needs only to contact the work at three places—six or so with a #07 or #08 plane (Figure 7-20). The points should be the full width of the sole and parallel (i.e., not twisted) to one another. Once three (or more) points contact a flat surface across the entire width of the sole, you are done with this stage. If you are ambitious, level the bottom beyond this point, flattening until the entire bottom has been polished (sometimes you

nearly have to anyway). Doing so, however, increases the chance of sanding the bottom out of flat, and of exceeding your own tolerance for tedium.

Start with any high areas between the intended contact surfaces, scraping or filing these until they appear to be slightly lower than the intended contact surfaces. Check frequently when using the scraper so that

Figure 7-20. Filing

Filing contact areas, maximum file contact

Filing areas between contact areas

Change direction often

A SCRAPER FOR METAL

A serviceable metal scraper can be made by grinding the end of a file to about a 60° bevel, then touching it up a bit with a diamond file. Push the scraper over the work or hold it nearly vertical and pull it with a scraping action.

The end of this old file has been ground to form a scraper for tuning the sole of a metal plane.

GAUGING STRAIGHTNESS

You can use feeler gauges under a straight edge to measure the amount a surface is out of flat, but it is easier to gauge the amount just by sighting under a straight edge: the human eye can see light through a gap of less than 0.001" (0.025mm).

AVOID DISTORTION

When checking your progress with a straightedge, always take the plane out of the vise or holding device so the clamping pressure does not distort it.

FILE MOUTH RELIEF

Before you start, file a little relief either side of the mouth to make sure the area does not contact the work after the sole is generally flattened.

you do not remove too much. Then move to the contact surfaces.

Try to lay the file simultaneously across two of the contact surfaces at any one time, keeping the file flat at all times and the pressure evenly distributed (Figure 7-20). Usually the file will be oriented along the length of the plane. Occasionally, if you have a particularly high spot, you can work across the width of the sole to concentrate on that spot and then turn the file along the length again to even up the surface. A good rule to follow is to have as much of the file in contact with the bottom of the plane as possible. Periodically vary the alignment of the file to avoid repetitive error.

As you file, bringing the contact surfaces into alignment, some of the areas in between—areas you want to be low, non-contact areas—may show themselves to be high, despite your previous efforts to lower them. You have two choices here. One, you could continue to file, enlarging these areas until the file contacts the reference planes

you are trying to bring into line. In such cases, you will have contact areas larger than you anticipated, which is okay. Alternatively, you could go back and put a little extra work on these areas to lower them and then return to bringing the contact areas into line. This whole process may happen several times before you are done.

Once you have satisfied yourself that the bottom is flat by checking with a straightedge, you can move to sandpaper. Sandpaper will not only smooth the marks from the filing, but the areas of polishing it leaves will in short order also tell you if the bottom is flat, or if you will have to go back to filing.

You can use wet/dry sandpaper, micron-graded plastic-backed abrasives, or adhesive-backed sandpaper. Tape (or adhere) one or two pieces (depending on the length of the plane and the size of abrasive sheet you are using) to a flat surface, such as a jointer bed. A granite platen is best but not necessary. Make sure your surface is flat. Simply because it is a milled surface such as a table saw, does not mean it is flat (my table saw is not, unfortunately).

If you do not have a machined surface you

can or want to use, a flat work top will do. Put a piece of ¼" (6mm) float glass over it to bridge any minor surface irregularities. (If the surface underneath the glass is not flat, the glass will flex under pressure.) Using water with wet/dry sandpaper will keep the paper from clogging and holds the sandpaper in place on a sheet of plate glass. Wet or dry, but especially wet, sanding will make a mess, so protect the surface you are working on. Start with 80- or 100-grit paper and work through at least 220- or 400-grit max. Once all your contact areas have been established with your coarsest grit, move to your next grit and then the next after a minimum of polishing: you do not want to remove any more iron than necessary. There is a danger that you can end up taking off more material from one side of the sole than the other. This will result in a number of headaches. Besides, cast iron is rather porous and will polish only so much anyway (Figure 7-21).

After leveling with the sandpaper, you may wish to further finesse the sole as described in Figure 7-22. You can carefully stroke these specific contact areas with a file the one to four strokes recommended to complete your configuration of the sole.

If you intend to use the plane on a shooting board one or both of the sides should be square to the sole. As before, do the major correction with scraper and file, finishing up with sandpaper on a platen to even things out. You can try to do this by using a block clamped square to the sandpaper surface, and although it is difficult to keep the plane

on the reference block and while applying pressure on the sandpaper, it can be useful for getting started. You do not need to flatten the entire side: once sufficient area has been straightened and squared to give consistent reference, you are done.

Figure 7-21. *Completed sole of a jack plane. The brighter areas have been filed and are slightly lower. The slightly darker areas are the major contact points and have been leveled and aligned by sanding on sandpaper on a granite platen. Completely removing the oval casting depression is not necessary.*

Figure 7-22. Schematic of Contact Areas of the Sole of Bailey-Style Planes

Contact areas extend the full width of the plane, are parallel, and are on a line with one another except where they have been relieved slightly as suggested in the illustration.

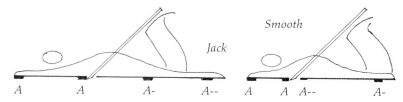

Areas in between contact areas are relieved only a few thousandths of an inch; A to A-: 1 or 2 file strokes; A to A--: 2 to 4 file strokes.

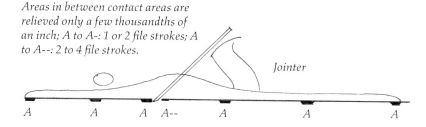

MOUTH GOING OUT OF PARALLEL

Taking too much off one side of the sole when flattening it can cause the mouth and back edge of the mouth opening at the frog to go out of parallel. The result is both go out of square with the length of the plane. This is because the relief angle and blade-bed angle are acute angles and not square to the sole, resulting in their diverging rapidly as material is removed from the sole.

Do not do this metal work on your bench!

The metal filings will infect your workpieces for years to come, not only dulling tools but showing up in the work, sometimes years later, as black dots or splotches, as the filings slowly rust.

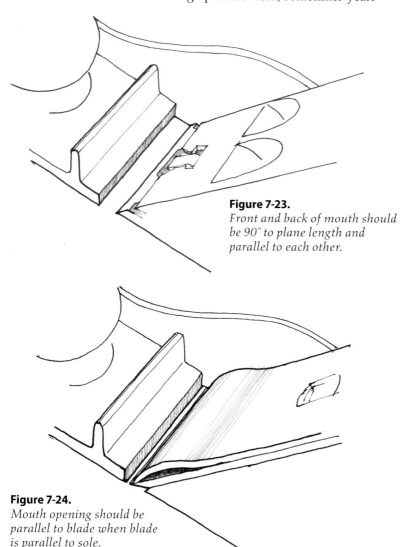

Figure 7-23.
Front and back of mouth should be 90° to plane length and parallel to each other.

Figure 7-24.
Mouth opening should be parallel to blade when blade is parallel to sole.

STEP 6: ADJUST THE MOUTH

Having finished the bottom, inspect the mouth. The mouth should be square to the length of the plane, straight, sharp where it meets the sole, and crisply formed (Figure 7-23). Insert the blade and chipbreaker assembly and the cap iron, and adjust the blade to a working position making sure the blade edge is square to the blade and parallel to the sole. The mouth opening should also be parallel to the blade edge—a factor more important than the mouth opening being square to the length of the plane (Figure 7-24). If the mouth opening is not parallel to the blade edge, adjust it with a file. The relief angle of the mouth opening should be 90° to 100°.

Carefully touch up the mouth with a file as needed. Go slow with this: you do not want to open up the mouth any more than you have to. It is hard to mark a line parallel to the blade and then file to the line dead straight. I suggest marking a line using a fine felt tip pen rather than a scribe, and then filing back into the line only as far as required to make the mouth parallel to what remains of the line. You will have to remove the blade to do this and then reinstall it—probably many times—to check your progress.

STEP 7: ATTEND TO THE DETAILS OF THE BODY AND SOLE

Gently smooth all of the edges around the bottom, making sure there are no sharp edges to mar the work. You do want the leading edge of the sole crisp, not rounded or sharp, as this helps keep shavings from riding under the plane as you work. Give the plane the once over and check for any other edges that might damage you or the work, and correct them with file or sandpaper.

Adjust the blade to make a light cut and make a trial shaving. If the bottom is truly flat, you should be able to make a shaving as thin as you want. (However, do not be misled by a board that is less flat than your plane bottom; the plane will only cut the high spots until the board is sufficiently, and incrementally, flattened.)

STEP 8: ATTEND TO THE DETAILS OF THE GRIP AND FINISH

I find it helpful to soften the slot of the screw that holds the front knob with a little sandpaper, and soften as well any mismatch of the screw to the front knob. This will reduce wear and tear on your hand. Now, unless you have a used plane with damaged handles, or want to refit the handles to your own specification, this completes the set-up of the plane. Your plane is ready to use.

ADJUSTING THE BAILEY-STYLE PLANE

Sighting down the sole of the plane, turn the wheel of the depth adjuster until the blade protrudes to your best guess of the intended amount. Push the lever of the lateral adjuster to make the blade parallel. Pushing the lever to the side of the blade that appears deeper will back off that side of the blade. This usually changes the depth of the blade, so it must be readjusted.

This is where it can get a bit aggravating, as it will take some spinning of the wheel to change direction. However, once you have about got it and take a trial stroke, you can fine-tune the blade depth in motion by turning the wheel in between strokes with your first finger without having to turn the plane over or change your grip **(Figure 1)**.

Day to day, there is no need to back the blade off or loosen the lever cap. You can return to the plane time after time at the same setting. However, if you put the plane into storage or do not use it for a long time, it is a good idea to loosen the lever cap and/or take the blade out, as the prolonged pressure of the lever cap eventually distorts the sole of the plane slightly, necessitating tuning up the sole. This has to be done periodically anyway (though it can usually go a long time between tune-ups), but the less often you will have to do this, the happier you will be.

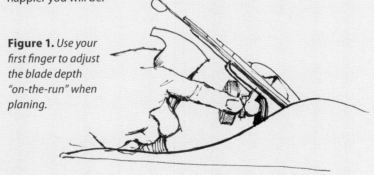

Figure 1. *Use your first finger to adjust the blade depth "on-the-run" when planing.*

SETTING UP A USED #6 FORE PLANE

Figures 1,2, and 3. *A flea-market find, $25. Rosewood handles caught my eye. No cracks (that I could see), not too worn, not rusted so badly it's pitted, corrugated sole, decent adjuster.*

Figures 4 and 5. *Surface rust on the blade and chipbreaker. It looked initially that the blade might be pitted (on the back— the worst place), but it turned out it was ok.*

Figure 6. *The space between the frog and the body was packed with shavings.*

Figure 7. *I disassembled all the screws and parts, cleaned them with a wire brush, oiled all the screws (luckily none were frozen), and put a coat of clear lacquer on the interior on the plane.*

SETTING UP A USED #6 FORE PLANE *(continued)*

Figure 8. *Bonus! The blade turned out to be laminated. You can see the two steels on the back of the blade, though I am unable to discern them on the bevel.*

The back of the blade took about 15–20 minutes: about 8 minutes lapping the back on the diamond stone and another 10+ minutes polishing it. I had inadvertently lifted the blade a couple of times, causing a slight rounding, which I then decided to take out, even though it would not affect the function of the blade.

The bevel took about 15 minutes: about 7 minutes carefully grinding the bevel back because of nicks, then another 7 or 8 minutes honing it.

Figure 9. *The chipbreaker, however, took a full half hour. It was typically heavily rounded and I filed a rather flat bevel in it to lower the hump. Unfortunately, the edge of the chipbreaker was not square to its length, so it took extra work to straighten it out, and get a good bottom edge-interface with the blade. Might end up getting an after-market chipbeaker.*

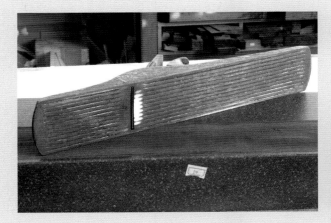

Figure 10. *Begin work on the sole. Four strokes on sandpaper reveal the major high spot to be under the frog. This is typical.*

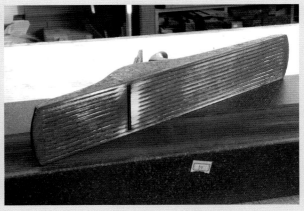

Figure 11. *Another 10 strokes on the sandpaper reveals that the throat is badly worn. A straight edge shows the mouth to be perhaps 0.01" low. This means that the entire rest of the sole must be brought down to this level. This is a lot of cast iron to remove.*

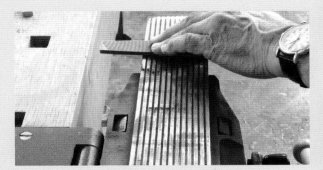

Figure 12. *Relief areas are filed between where I want the contact areas so there is less metal for the sandpaper to remove.*

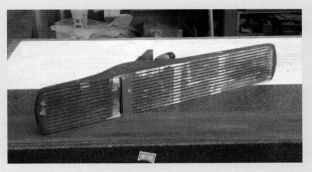

Figure 13. *Ten sanding strokes, 3 minutes of filing and another 30 sanding strokes shows the contact areas emerging. Still a lot of work to do at the mouth.*

Figure 14. *Filing the contact areas to bring them into line.*

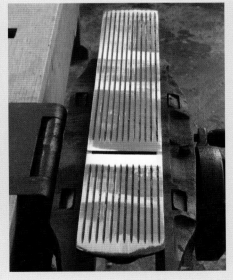

Figure 15. *Eight minutes of filing and 20 sanding strokes and we're in pretty good shape. A number of points on the one side are higher, particularly right behind the blade, and though the area in front of the mouth is flat almost to the mouth now, it is still a bit rounded: it would be best if sharp.*

Figure 16 and 17. *Reflection on the sole was suggesting that the bottom might have a bit of twist, or a low corner. Checking with winding sticks showed that the front corner was a bit low, though the rest of the plane was flat.*

SETTING UP A USED #6 FORE PLANE *(continued)*

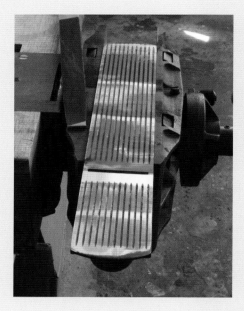

Figure 18. *Four segments of filing for around 4 minutes each alternating with 10 to 15 sanding strokes and we're in pretty good shape.*

Figures 19 and 20. *Filing the mouth. It was neither straight nor smooth, though it was basically square. I filed it at a bit of an angle to give added chip clearance when the mouth is closed tight.*

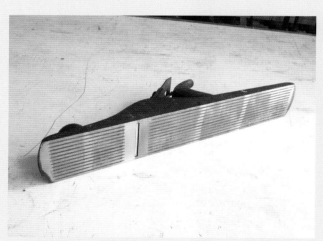

Figure 21. *The completed sole.*

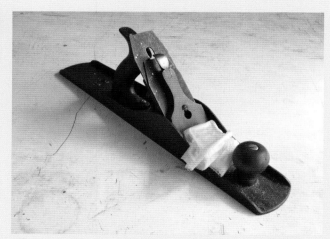

Figure 22. *Ready to go to work.*

If you have a #3 or #4 and it's not in too bad shape, you may be able to use sandpaper for the whole process. However, if the plane is worn at the mouth or is a large plane—or worse, a large plane worn at the mouth—you will have to intervene with file or scraper. The area of the sole of a #4 is about 20 square inches; the area of a fore plane is nearly 54 square inches, and is geometrically more work to flatten. Using sandpaper for the whole process, as I have experienced teaching classes, will result in a distorted sole and probably a distorted enthusiasm for woodworking.

Setting Up the Stanley #60½

If you buy a new Bailey 60½ (low angle, bevel-up) block plane made by Stanley or one of its mid-market competitors, or a used or vintage version, you're going to have to do some work on it. The new, larger versions of the bevel-up planes, however, are better made and you should have to do little to them. But the procedures for checking out both planes are similar.

With this plane, unlike bevel-down planes, I would wait to prepare the blade. Assuming it is square (check it!), you can use it as a reference for squaring the mouth edge.

Check the blade bed behind the mouth for irregularities: a bit or enamel, flash or a corner that was not fully milled. Remove the offender carefully; you're really not going to be able to correct the blade bed accurately, so I wouldn't do more than this.

Many versions of the Stanley #60½ plane have a shortcoming endemic to the plane, and you might also want to check larger versions of bevel-up planes for the same problem. On some versions the lever cap is so short that it clamps the blade behind the lower bed surface, potentially bending the blade so the edge is raised and not in contact with the bed. This could result in chattering. If your plane chatters and your bevel angle is correct for the work you're doing, you can change the blade for an after-market blade that's thicker and/or file the lever cap screw slot a little longer so the lever cap moves down closer to the blade edge when clamped.

Remove the mouthpiece. Clean it and its seat carefully. Reinstall it and check to see if it moves freely and sits flush with the sole. On these mid-market planes, the mouthpiece is punched out of sheet stock: where the shear enters the metal it starts clean, but the metal ruptures as the shear exits. This leaves a rough edge where it moves in the plane body, causing it to stick. The two sides that contact the plane body should be carefully filed until it moves freely enough to be easily adjusted back and forth its full range. You have to keep these two edges square and parallel; check every stroke or two for fit and squareness.

Reinstall the mouthpiece and the blade. Adjust the blade so that it protrudes slightly (less than ¹⁄₆₄") and is *parallel to the sole*. Looking down from the top of the plane into the light, adjust the mouthpiece until it almost touches the blade. It should be straight and parallel to the blade's edge. Also check it with a square. You're going to have to remove the mouthpiece to file it and repeatedly test fit it to get it. When you're done the mouth should be sharp, straight, 90° to the sole, square to the plane, and parallel to the blade when the blade is parallel to the sole.

Back the blade off ¹⁄₁₆" and check the sole for flatness. Prepare the sole using techniques described in the section before on bevel-down planes.

ADJUSTING THE THROAT

You adjust the throat by holding the plane up to the light, looking down into the top so that the light shines through the throat. A fine, but properly adjusted, mouth opening will show a barely perceptible—but uniform—opening. It will be the same width all the way across, not tapering. If it touches in one or more spots, the mouth or the blade is not straight or they are not parallel. Both the mouth and the blade must be square to the length of the plane when the cutting edge is parallel to the sole.

Check the sides for square. This plane is a good candidate for use on a shooting board, so it is helpful to have the sides square to the sole. Besides, on these mid-market planes, the sanding of the surface is so rough it almost begs to be smoothed. To check the sole for square, lay the plane on its side on a flat surface and put a square to the sole. This will give a clearer reading than checking directly on the plane. If it's off by very much, begin by using a file, then finishing with sandpaper as with the sole.

The lever cap is often a rough casting with a rough edge that bears on the blade when clamped down. It seems that filing the underside of this bearing edge straight and smooth would be an improvement, but I'm not sure it is necessary. Also, on the plane I bought the blade adjustment knob was not fully driven on the threaded shaft, and required three or four full turns to engage the blade before I could begin to adjust it. If this is the case with yours, unscrew it out of the plane and set the threaded end on a block of wood (so you don't damage the threads) and tap the knob with a mallet to fully seat it.

Go around the plane and soften the edges so they don't mar the wood (or you). Keep a crisp front edge to help keep shavings from riding up under the plane while working.

Setting Up Rabbet Planes

The same procedures, in the same order, are followed when setting up the rabbet plane (Figure 7-25) as when setting up a bench plane. Some things, however, are done a little differently, as follows.

STEP 1. INSPECT THE PLANE

Large portions of a rabbet-plane body are often cut away to provide chip clearance or to allow the blade to do its job. Check for cracks at all narrowed portions of the plane, especially if there is pressure associated with them (such as from the lever cap or wedge). Cracks in a metal plane will render it useless. Also, check that the sole and two adjacent sides are square to each other. Reject any plane that is not square.

The most important thing to know about a rabbet plane is that the blade must be able to protrude on its cutting side(s) about $\frac{1}{64}$" (0.4mm) or maybe a little less. This seems counterintuitive, but unless the blade protrudes slightly, the plane will step away from the cut line as the cut deepens, resulting in an out-of-square shoulder and a generally narrower rabbet. Perhaps this is due to the additive effect of the slight springback of the wood that happens with each cut. Check, when you first get the plane, that the blade is slightly wider than the plane body. (The check is not necessary on a one-sided rabbet plane, obviously. Just make sure the blade can be positioned proud of the side.)

If for some reason the blade exceeds $\frac{1}{64}$" (0.4mm) on both cutting sides (unlikely on a metal plane), then the blade can be carefully ground narrower. If the blade is too

Figure 7-25.
The Clifton 3-in-1 plane disassembled: chisel plane, bull-nose piece, and rabbet-plane nosepiece.

narrow you will have to get a new blade or a new plane. While the blade can sometimes be pushed to the working side to accommodate a too-narrow blade, there is no reason to have to deal with it on a recently acquired plane. And if the blade cannot be pushed to the side, tilting the blade toward that side is not a satisfactory solution. Both the blade and the plane are ground square and tilting the blade puts the edge out of parallel with the sole.

STEP 2. PREPARE THE BLADE

After inspecting your plane—and establishing that you have the correct width blade—begin setting it up by sharpening the blade. As described in "Prepare the Blade" on page 96, flatten the back first. The bevel must then be sharpened straight across, no curvature, and must be square enough to its length so it can be made parallel to the sole within the plane's range of adjustment (usually not very much). With a skewed-blade rabbet plane, you will have to establish (or maintain) the correct angle of the blade to accomplish the same parallel relation to the sole. You will not be able to check it with a square; so, if you have lost the correct angle, it may take some putting it in and out of the plane to get it right.

STEP 3. PREPARE AND FIT THE CHIPBREAKER (IF THERE IS ONE)

If there is a chipbreaker, fitting it is pretty much the same as with the bench plane. You can refer to the general procedures in "Prepare the Chipbreaker" on page 99 and to the set-up section specific to your style of plane.

STEP 4. BED THE BLADE PROPERLY

Inspect the blade bed for flaws. I strongly suggest you do not touch this area on a metal plane, because it is difficult to access and easy to mess up. If you have a flaw, return the plane and get another.

STEP 5. CONFIGURE THE SOLE

I usually do not attempt to condition the sole of a metal rabbet plane for two reasons. First, the bottom does not need to be as flat as that of a fine smooth plane, because this plane is for shaping rather than smoothing wood. Second, it is easy to lose square between the sides and the sole in trying to flatten either. If the sides are not square to the sole, I suggest you return the plane.

If, however, the plane cannot make a fine cut even though you can see the blade protrude, probably the blade bed area is depressed slightly under pressure of the lever cap. This is an inescapable weak spot in rabbet planes. First make sure the lever cap is only tight enough to secure the blade: in fact, back it off to a point you think is too loose and use it. If it slips, then tighten it a bit; continue doing this until the blade has sufficient pressure. It's important to not over-tighten the lever cap as this can not only distort the bottom, but actually break the plane, usually at the lever cap pivot point, or the blade bed.

Under working pressure, with the blade backed off, check the bottom with a straight edge held up to the light. If backing the pressure off slightly on the lever cap doesn't solve the problem, you will have to carefully sand the bottom until it is flat. Proceed carefully, using single controlled strokes in one direction and inspecting the bottom every couple of strokes, both for progress and for squareness all along its length. You can rig up a guide, such as a block of wood clamped square to the stone, but don't count on it: still check it every couple of strokes. Stop as soon as there are sanding scratches all the way up to the throat, indicating you can now take as fine a shaving as you want.

STEP 6. ADJUST THE MOUTH

On a metal rabbet plane with a fixed mouth, you are stuck with what you get. Correcting a badly formed or abused mouth will be unproductive, and closing it down impractical. On a plane with an adjustable mouth, you can, of course,

adjust the mouth tighter. Just make sure the parts stay in alignment when they are moved (though this is going to be tough to correct if these parts are not milled right). Again, squaring up the mouth is difficult; and I would only consider doing it on a good quality old plane, and then only if I needed the plane to be able to produce a finish surface as opposed to correcting a rabbet. I would not accept an out-of-square mouth on a new plane.

STEP 7. ATTEND TO THE DETAILS OF THE BODY AND SOLE

Rabbet planes have a strong tendency to jam with chips (bench and block planes are mercifully free of this problem). The solution can be as simple as frequently pushing the shaving out the exit hole—sometimes as often as every stroke of the plane. This can become a little annoying, but if you forget to do it, the consequence is worse: the shavings become tightly jammed, and clearing them entails a prolonged struggle. And it becomes even more frustrating when you have to do this repeatedly. I don't have a solution for this; it's just endemic to the plane.

You shouldn't have much else to do on a decent plane, unless you come across an errant sharp edge. I do recommend that whenever you are done using it you rub it down with camelia oil to keep it from staining from hand oils, and also to lubricate it for the next time.

SETTING UP A NEW STANLEY #60½

Figure 1. *I picked up a new Stanley #60 ½ at my local contractor supply house. It came in a clear plastic bubble package, dressed to go to work. The plane appeared to be a rather rough sandcasting that had been enameled over. The sole and sides were coarsely sanded, probably with 80 grit—but they were flat; that is, not rounded at the ends as often happens with poorly sanded pieces.*

Figure 2. *The blade bed and recess for the mouthpiece were milled well enough. The blade bed is small and the blade rests at the top on the adjuster rather than directly on any cast iron, as you can see in this comparison with the Veritas (center), and the Lie-Nielsen (right). This is perhaps not fair as the Stanley cost about a third of what the others cost and has been made this way, successfully, for over a hundred years.*

Figure 3. *The throat piece was punched and so its edges were torn as the piece exited the sheet. This rough edge prevented the mouthpiece from moving smoothly and had to be filed. It took only 4 careful, full length and square cuts with a file each side to correct this. You want this to fit snugly with no play.*

Figure 4. *The mouthpiece reinstalled. You can see the coarseness of the overall sanding in this photo.*

SETTING UP A NEW STANLEY #60½ *(continued)*

Figure 5. *Ten strokes on the sandpaper. The sole is high on both ends, making no contact at the mouth area, where you want it to.*

Figure 6. *Three minutes of filing the area between the front of the sole and the mouth as well as the area behind the mouth where the blade bed is, and 2 minutes of sanding. The area at the mouth is not yet making contact.*

Figure 7. *Five more minutes of filing and 2 more minutes of sanding, and we now have sufficient contact. This plane could be used now. About 15 minutes to this point. But I'm going to try and refine it some more.*

Figure 8. *Filing the relief area between the front of the plane and the mouth.*

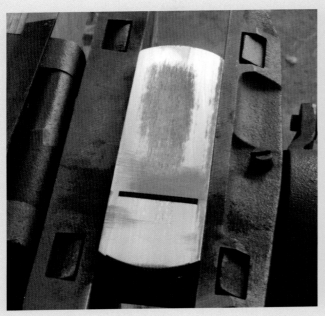

Figure 9. *Filing the relief area behind the mouth in the area of the blade bed, a troublesome spot.*

Figure 10. *After about three minutes of filing.*

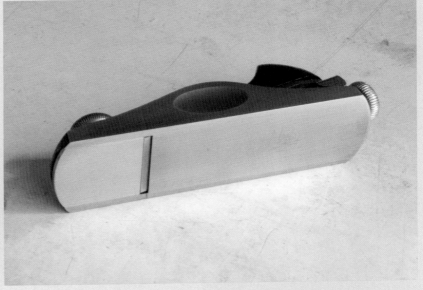

Figure 11. *After about 40 strokes of sanding. The area behind the mouth under the bed is still low from the filing, though the left side (in this photo) behind the bed is still in contact. The depression in the casting under the upper part of the blade bed also remains. Notice all along the right-hand edge the roughness in the casting that remains.*

Figure 12. *I wanted to reduce the rough spot left from shrinkage of the casting at the extra thickness of the upper blade bed (it was probably milled before the casting had fully aged, resulting in the low spot with the same finish as the rest of the sole), so I continued filing and sanding for about another 15-20 minutes. This was not actually necessary for a functioning plane.*

SETTING UP A NEW STANLEY #60½ (continued)

Figure 13. *The mouthpiece as it came. You can see the roughness as a result of being punched out of piece of sheet steel. One edge is clean, the other torn. Unfortunately, the torn edge faces the work and needs to be straight and sharp. Careful work with a file fixed that. To check the mouthpiece for square you must put the blade in the plane, under pressure, and adjust the blade so that the edge is parallel to the sole of the plane. Then adjust the mouthpiece until it almost touches the blade. The light gap between the two should be parallel. If not, remove the mouthpiece, and carefully file the edge of the mouth until it is. Only file 3 or 4 strokes before checking. Don't be tempted to file a lot without checking.*

Figure 14. *It's good practice to make the sides of the plane square to the sole. It's absolutely necessary if you plan to use the plane on a shooting board. After checking for square, begin the process by filing the offending high point, then finishing on the sandpaper.*

Figure 15. *Check the side for square by laying the plane on its side and and putting the square to the sole, rather than putting the square on the plane itself. Check frequently when sanding.*

Figure 16. *Works pretty well.*

Troubleshooting

Using a handplane can be immensely rewarding, but it is not without its frustrations. Sometimes it seems you have done everything right but your results are still disappointing, or inconsistent. I cannot begin to answer all the questions you will ask yourself while you work, but a review of the information contained in this book should answer most of them. I will try to answer some basic questions here I hope will tie information together and send you in the right direction when analyzing a problem.

Problem: The blade leaves a series of repeated parallel marks on the work, perpendicular to the stroke of the plane.

This is called *blade chatter* and happens because the blade or blade edge is flexing under pressure of the cut. The edge digs deeper into the wood until the blade's resistance to bending exceeds the resistance of the wood, and the blade springs back up. At that the blade reengages the wood, begins to flex, and the process happens all over again. Blade chatter happens primarily because the blade is not fully supported at the heel of the bevel, or because the bevel angle is too small (and thus the metal leading to the edge is too thin). There are a number of things to check, in the following order:

1. Check that the blade is bedded properly. Check that nothing is between the blade and the frog: sometimes when you reinstall a blade after sharpening, for instance, an errant piece of shaving is trapped under the blade. Make sure every time you replace the blade after sharpening that the frog is clean. Also, it is possible the frog was badly machined and the blade cannot seat properly. Check again for any irregularities. Also, be certain the frog is securely screwed down and unable to be rocked.

It is also possible the frog is misadjusted. If it is too far back, the blade will ride up off the frog and be part on the body casting and part on the frog. If it is too far forward, the blade will not be supported at the very heel of the bevel. Or, if it is not parallel to the main body casting, the blade will be lifted up on one corner (see Figures 7-12, 7-13, and 7-14 on page 103). Also, make sure the blade is properly set on the adjuster nib; otherwise, the blade will be prevented from bedding properly. You can usually tell this right away, however, because the cam lever on the cap iron (lever cap) will be noticeably more difficult, if not impossible, to engage. If your cap iron tightens with a screw, you will not be able to tell without physically checking.

2. The second most probable cause of blade chatter, and probably the primary suspect on a well set-up plane, is the bevel angle. If the bevel angle is too small, the bevel itself will flex and cause chatter. "Too small," however, is relative. The bevel angle must be appropriate for the depth of cut, the blade (cutting) angle, and the type of wood. For instance, a bevel angle may be just barely sufficient for a certain depth of cut, but may begin to chatter if set deeper, or if used to plane a harder wood.

Another important factor related to the bevel angle is sharpness: When a blade dulls, it encounters greater resistance to the cut, causing the edge to flex down and begin to chatter. You may notice this in the midst of working, the same plane that has been cutting well on the same piece of wood starts chattering and the only thing that has changed is the sharpness of your edge. This means your bevel angle on this blade is at the limit of its performance. You will have to keep this blade very sharp, or increase the bevel angle. If you suspect that the bevel angle is incorrect, or too small for the work you are doing, reconsider and adjust your bevel angles (see "Bevel Angle" on page 50 and "The Correct Bevel Angle" on page 50.

3. Another, but less likely, cause of chatter is a poorly designed and manufactured blade and chipbreaker. This is a problem inherent in Bailey/Stanley planes. You can check "Chipbreakers" on page 42 for a discussion of this problem. Yet, a thin modern blade is not necessarily condemned to chatter; these blades often perform without problems. But a thin blade, a thin chipbreaker that forces that blade into an arch lifting most of it off the bed, and a cap iron that does not set the blade assembly fully to the blade bed, constitutes a setup prone to problems. Add to this a chipbreaker set to the edge, a frog adjusted forward restricting the mouth opening, a deep cut—or especially any of these in combination—and the potential for chatter is high.

If you believe the blade bed is satisfactory and you have an appropriate bevel angle, but are still getting some chatter, it may be

the thin, arched blade assembly, and you may want to upgrade to a thicker blade, and possibly a better chipbreaker. A more substantial blade assembly will more likely remain flat and fully bedded. If there is insufficient room at the mouth to use a thicker blade, then you can only upgrade the chipbreaker, to something like a Clifton Sta-Set model, which sits flat on the blade.

Problem: I cannot cut as fine a shaving as I want. The plane goes from a cut slightly too deep to no cut at all.

Either your plane or the work is not flat enough. Check the plane first—you probably have missed some area on the sole when you tuned-up the plane. This is easy to do. Go back and check it again.

The other factor is the work. If the work is not sufficiently well prepared (not flat

KEEP YOUR EYES ON THE PRIZE

The goal here is to get a beautiful surface suitable for the chosen finish and position of the piece in the work, in the most efficient manner possible. This is not an academic exercise. On the other hand, when you are learning about planes and trying to improve your skills, a little extra effort trying to figure out what is going on before turning to scrapers and sandpaper will be rewarded in the end. Ultimately, you have to decide when handplaning is no longer the most productive solution. Learning to make that decision is also part of the acquisition of skills.

enough), you may have to set the blade deeper than you want to get the plane to cut even intermittent areas of the surface. If your plane does cut a fine shaving here and there, or maybe even at only one small place, then the problem probably is in the preparation of the work. You should go back and prepare it better.

Problem: I get tearout.

Using the information in this book, you should be able to see markedly improved results in the performance of your planes; with practice I hope you will find yourself planing woods and getting results you hadn't previously thought possible—and also knowing when to put down the plane and head for the scrapers and sandpaper.

The setup of the plane is critical: a large portion of the skill required for effective planning resides here. Technique adds to this effectiveness, but does not substitute it for it.

To reduce tearout, first, sharpen the blade. Match the blade steel to the work and make it *sharp*. Use an appropriate blade pitch (if you can), adjust the chipbreaker and mouth opening to restrain the shaving, and use as light a cut as you can for the stage of the work.

If your plane and the surface of the work is well prepared, you can usually get good, reliable, tearout-free results on the final surfacing in most woods, though there will be those pieces that defy your best efforts. It is much easier to get tearout-free results when the plane is set for a fine cut, but in order for

KEEP THE SURFACE FLAT

Do not get distracted with localized problems. You must plane the entire surface the same amount—difficult areas as well as straightforward—in order to maintain flat. Otherwise, not only will the surface appear irregular but also the plane will begin to bridge the troubled areas by riding on the adjacent, less planed surfaces. These higher areas will then have to be planed down in line with the low areas before you can go any further.

this to work, the surface must be ready for a fine cut, that is, properly prepared.

Avoiding tearout is a much bigger problem when preparing stock because preparing stock means removing a lot of wood, which necessitates a deeper cut, with the chipbreaker and mouth opening set back accordingly. The setup, of course, diminishes the effectiveness of these two major tactics in eliminating tearout. As preparation proceeds, you can gradually adjust the chipbreaker and mouth openings down to restrict the shaving, also taking a lighter cut. At each stage of the preparation you want to see tearout improve, aiming for its total elimination by the final smoothing.

Avoiding tearout also entails reading the wood and changing directions accordingly as you move across the surface. You learn the character of your wood as you plane, and you respond. Curly areas that change direction in the middle of the board may necessitate rotating the plane as you approach that area, to change the angle of attack, and then rotating it back again. Planing adjacent boards where the grain direction changes at the glue line often requires that you plane along the glue line in each direction without bridging the joint. Holding the plane at a bit of a diagonal localizes the cut a bit more and sometimes helps to be able to skirt along the joint.

Tearout hotspots notwithstanding, you should plane the entire surface in overlapping strokes across the width and length of the piece and back again. If you finish with scraping and sanding, do not be tempted to give trouble areas extra strokes, as this will distort the surface and be readily visible after the finish goes on.

A technique both Westerners and Japanese use is to dampen the surface of the wood with a wet rag to soften the wood fibers. This supposedly allows the fibers to be sheared cleanly. I have had indifferent results trying this, and I suspect that it is not going to work in all woods, particularly those that prefer a higher cutting angle. I think it is worth further experimentation, however.

Problem: The mouth of the plane jams with chips.

First, take the blade out of the plane and check to see if the chips are jamming in the mouth itself, or at or under the chipbreaker. The chips may appear to be jamming at the mouth when in reality they are jamming at the chipbreaker and backing up to fill the mouth. This is the more likely occurrence.

If the chips are jamming between the chipbreaker and the blade, and not actually at the mouth, the chipbreaker's fit to the blade must be tuned so that it fits tight. The underside edge of the chipbreaker where it meets the blade must be straight, and slightly undercut (Figure 7-6, on page 100). The chipbreaker also must be formed so it puts sufficient pressure at the interface between it and the blade to keep chips from forcing their way in.

If all of these are tuned up and chips still find their way in between the blade and chipbreaker, then possibly the edge of the blade is flexing under the pressure of the cut and opening up a gap between it and the chipbreaker. The bevel is flexing because it is too small (and thus the metal leading to the edge is too thin); or the blade is flexing because it is not properly supported. Sometimes the chipbreaker is rigid enough— but not tight enough—to allow a badly supported blade or too-thin edge to flex independently of it. Check the bevel angle of the blade and consider regrinding it to a larger one if it appears questionable. As well, check the blade seat and make sure the blade is fully supported. Correct these and verify that the chipbreaker has enough pressure on the edge to maintain contact under working conditions (Figure 7-9, on page 100).

Chips will also jam at the mouth of the plane itself because sometimes there is insufficient clearance. Check that the blade is not set deeper than slightly less than the width of the mouth opening. Also, check the throat opening and the upper surface of the chipbreaker to make sure there is sufficient clearance between the opening and all points of the chipbreaker. Sometimes if tolerances are very close, a blade will flex down into the wood in use and take a deeper chip than it was set for—than what the mouth or throat opening will accept. This is actually blade chatter, but since it happens only once and jams instead of leaving chatter marks, it is hard to diagnose this as the blade or blade edge flexing. If all the tolerances look sufficient, then check the bevel angle and blade support.

Problem: The plane leaves tracks or ridges in the work.

Rotate the work so the light source shines parallel to the work surface. Look closely and see if it is a ridge or a step. If it is a ridge, then you have a nick in the blade. You will have to go back and re-sharpen.

If the track is a step, then one or both corners of the blade are set too deep for the shape of the blade. You need to back the blade off or adjust the lateral adjuster until the blade no longer leaves steps. If it no longer

cuts, then you need to either flatten the bottom of the plane some more or prepare the work better as described above. Check the different sections for the appropriate blade shape for the plane you are using.

Problem: The plane seems to leave shiny streaks on the work.

These are usually burnishing marks from some slightly higher spot on the sole of the plane. The most likely culprit is the area just to either side of the blade opening, since these are easy to neglect. This is why I relieve these areas on my planes; however, other missed spots on the sole can do this as well. Also, sometimes shavings can collect at the mouth (especially at the corners), pack tightly, and cause burnishing.

8

SHARPENING PLANE BLADES

A Basic Skill that Leads to Others

I have two goals when sharpening:

- the acquisition and improvement of skills (sharpening and otherwise)

- getting back to working wood as quickly as possible—with the most effective blade edge.

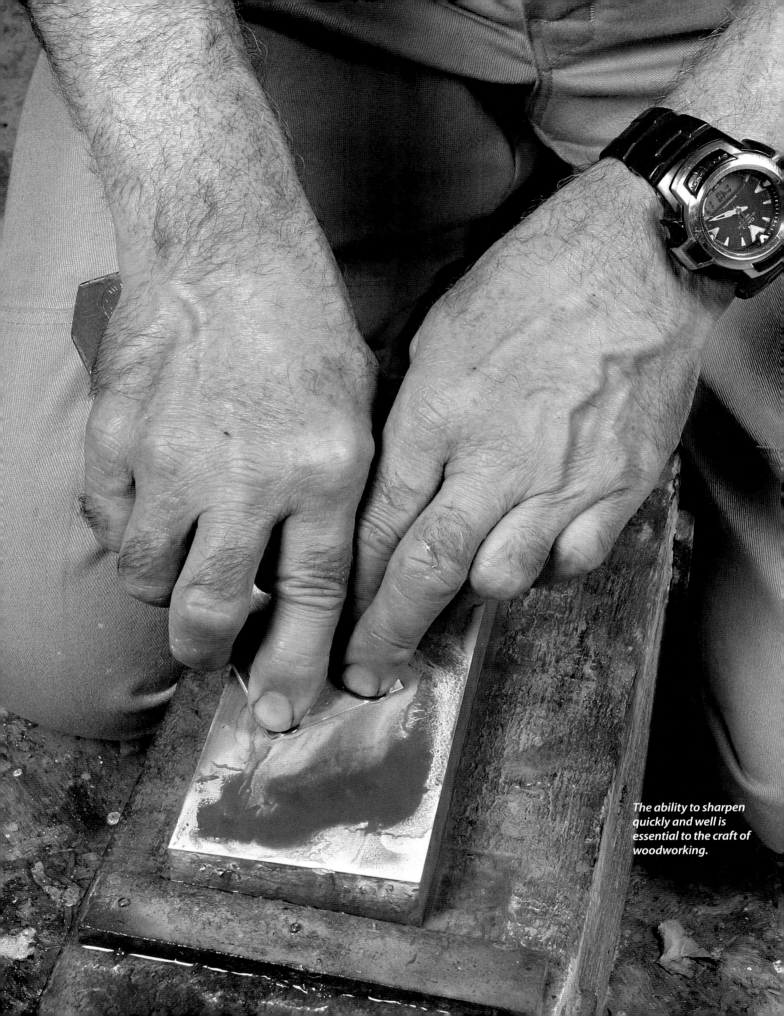

The ability to sharpen quickly and well is essential to the craft of woodworking.

SHARPENING IS FUNDAMENTAL

Sharpening is fundamental to the craft of woodworking. Learning to sharpen fast and effectively lays the foundation for the acquisition of nearly all of the other skills required for the craft. It teaches body mechanics and the art of working efficiently. It teaches you how to focus both your attention and your efforts for maximum productivity. It teaches you to see, and what to look for. It teaches you to feel—to feel your own rhythms, the material, and the feedback from the tool—less smooth, smoother, smoothest, sharp, and sharper.

In some woodworking traditions, the first real woodworking task given to the apprentice was sharpening tools. Only when the apprentice could demonstrate he could produce an adequate edge did the master judge his skills and his knowledge were sufficient to proceed. The acquisition of skills begins with sharpening.

Because of the importance of sharpening in teaching body mechanics and the art of working efficiently, I always strongly encourage woodworkers to sharpen without a jig. (I have other reasons as well.) This is where woodworkers learn to make each motion pay off. Through sharpening, woodworkers learn:

- The edge is not scrubbed back and forth across the stone but rather stroked with direct intention each time it is moved.
- There is clear focus of effort, pressure, and attention at the cutting edge itself, not the bevel.
- While the bevel does remain flat, not rocking on the stone, it is the edge of that bevel being sharpened, and which must be zeroed into with both the mind and the body.

Learning this and how to do it, and how to do it each time, makes it easier to understand that:

- Sawing is not a tiring repetition of frantic arm motion, but a series of individual strokes, each advancing the cut on the shoulder of the scribe line, and to the maximum amount the wood and the cut of the saw will allow;
- Clearing waste for a dovetail or mortise with a chisel is a series of distinct, clean, and precise cuts of exactly the same amount, to the line, so waste is cleanly excavated the first time to its final shape (though perhaps not its final size);
- Each stroke of the plane is individual, dependent on the grain of the wood at that particular place, the angle of attack, your speed, your body position, the diminishing sharpness of the blade, and your increasing fatigue.

Understanding this—and eventually, with mindful practice, internalizing this—each stroke of the plane, the chisel, or the saw produces optimal results, and the work proceeds quickly.

JIG DRAWBACKS

Use a sharpening jig and your energy is dissipated, half of it going to the roller, half to the bevel, and very little going directly to the edge of the blade, which is where all of your energy should be going. The roller becomes a blindfold, obscuring your interaction with the edge you are sharpening. It keeps you from learning the feel of the bevel sitting flat on the stone as you stroke it; from learning to focus your attention at the edge while keeping the bevel flat to the stone; and from learning not to rock or lean, yet produce maximum results at that cutting edge, where you want it.

All of this ties into my second goal: getting back to working wood. Because the jig dissipates both your energy and your focus, effort is wasted and time is lost. It is slower, and it is disruptive. Add to that the problem of jigging the blade to the exact position in the apparatus—because if it is not exact, you create a new bevel on the blade when you go to sharpen—and your time and tedium increase exponentially.

Learn to sharpen with the attention of the mind and body focused to your fingertips, because in the end, this will be how you will be doing woodworking. Yes, there is a learning curve, but really, woodworking is just one big learning curve. The challenges woodworking offers is one of its appeals. You can take a shortcut, but it will catch up

to you later. Time invested here will serve you throughout your further woodworking endeavors.

Bevel Shape

Three bevel configurations can be used on a sharpened blade:

• Flat

• Hollow-ground

• Micro bevel

Traditional sources I have seen emphasize that the bevel must be flat for several reasons. First, it gives maximum support to the edge while allowing the thinnest possible bevel. A rounded bevel, usually a result of rocking the blade when sharpening, results in a much thicker bevel angle at the cutting edge, even though the average of the bevel overall may be the intended angle. This results in the blade ceasing to cut at the least bit of dulling, as the bevel behind the edge begins to rub and suspend the edge from the work. A hollow-ground blade undercuts the edge leaving little material to support it. It actually undercuts it more than you think because the actual angle is that of the tangent of the hollow just behind the edge. This is much smaller than the angle the blade was ground to and often results in a support angle behind the edge of much less than the 20° to 22°, generally considered to be the absolute minimum practical bevel angle (see page 50). This may or may not be a problem.

Telltale signs the bevel is a problem are:

- Chattering (even though properly bedded, the undercut metal leading to the edge is flexing under the load);
- Clogging at the mouth or throat of a properly adjusted plane (the blade—not sufficiently supported by the bevel—is flexing down under the load, enlarging the mouth, causing it to cut a shaving larger than the opening can accommodate);
- Clogging between the blade and the chipbreaker, even though the chipbreaker is fitted properly (again, the blade's thin edge is flexing under the load and opening a gap between it and the chipbreaker).

A flat bevel provides the thinnest possible edge with the greatest support behind that edge. If any of these problems show up with a flat bevel, it is because the bevel is ground at too small an angle, a geometry that is plain to see and easy to deal with. Laminated blades are honed to a flat bevel, as the hard, brittle steel is too vulnerable without the support of the bevel behind it.

Besides its potential functional problems, I have always believed the hollow grind presents maintenance problems as well. A grinding wheel leaves deep scratches, many of which seem to remain even after establishing a brightly honed bevel. To ensure they no longer remain near the edge, I always give the bevel a few extra strokes on the first sharpening stone. However, waterstones cut so fast—much faster than

the old oil or Arkansas stones—that this nearly eliminates the hollow, especially on an unlaminated carbon-steel blade. After two or three sharpenings, the hollow has been honed away. I could never understand the point of taking the time to regrind the hollow when the waterstones cut so fast. Let's get back to working wood.

There are some occasions, however, when I purposely establish a hollow grind, even if an edge does not have to be reshaped (because of a nick, for instance). The primary reason is to take the hump out of a rounded bevel. Sometimes, after a number of honings, I just lose it. The bevel is simply too rounded to easily flatten. In such a case I put it on a grinding wheel and hollow-grind the area between the edge and the heel of the bevel. I do not take it all the way out to the edge, both for expediency, and to avoid possibly overheating the edge. I grind away just enough so that the blade sits flat on the sharpening stone and does not rock. I can then easily hone the blade to a flat, unrounded bevel. At the first honing, however, I do not necessarily take the time to fully remove the hollow left by the grinder. I just hone until the edge is sharpened. If a bit of the hollow remains, it is not enough to compromise the functioning of the blade, and it will be gone soon enough in the next honing or two, anyway.

The micro bevel is, again, a maintenance issue with me. The micro bevel gives a good edge the first time. The next time you sharpen, you have two choices: (1) sharpen only the micro bevel, or (2) sharpen the whole bevel and the micro bevel. If you sharpen only the micro bevel, after two or three sharpenings, you will have a macro bevel. You will have lost all of the advantage of a micro bevel, and you have a main bevel that is rapidly developing a rounded profile. If you hone the main bevel to get the best edge, you must hone it all the way out to the edge, not just to the beginning of the microbevel. Then, putting a micro bevel on the blade at this point is just redoing work.

Anyway, if you hone without a guide (as I recommend), some slight variation in the bevel angle is unavoidable. In addition, with proper technique you can make this work for you. By rotating the blade edge orientation to perpendicular to the length of the sharpening stone on your final stone, rather than using the approximate 45° orientation that gives the most stability when sharpening, you assume a position of higher risk (Figure 8-1). The slight increase in inaccuracy will ensure the edge itself is polished and slightly bolstered.

I believe many of these elaborate systems—hollow grinding, micro bevels, jigs—do not address one of the main issues of sharpening: its frequency. If you are using your planes to their maximum benefit, for periods, at least, you may have to resharpen several times a day—maybe every 15 or

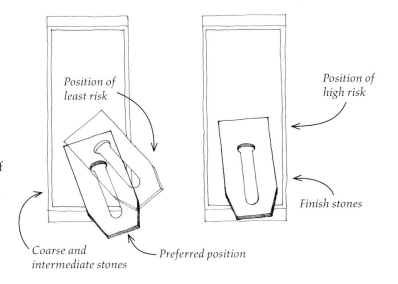

Figure 8-1. Positions of Risk

Position of least risk

Position of high risk

Finish stones

Coarse and intermediate stones

Preferred position

20 minutes at some point in some projects. Fiddling with contraptions and a variety of angles each time consumes too much time and is distracting. Without all this stuff, but with a good set of stones and a properly established bevel angle, you can be back to woodworking after three or four minutes at the stones, which is sometimes less than the amount of time it would take to get a jig properly attached.

Grinding

I was once told never to grind a Japanese blade. Boy, getting out a nick in a blade without a grinder can be very Zen. I became enlightened, however, when a Japanese chisel maker told me that, yes you can grind a Japanese blade on a grinding wheel—with the proper technique. The technique is simply to keep a finger directly behind the bevel, as close to the grinding wheel as possible. When the blade becomes too hot for your finger, it is too hot for the blade, and grinding pauses (Figure 8-2).

NOT JUST JAPANESE BLADES

This brings up an important issue. Not just Japanese blades are sensitive to the stress of grinding. Treat any good blade in the same manner. While a grinding wheel can easily draw the temper of an edge, aggressively grinding, stopping just short of color change, quenching, and then regrinding, causes noticeable structural change in the edge, especially when combined with quenching, which itself can cause microscopic cracking. All of this degrades the edge, reducing the cutting ability and life of the edge.

Alloy steel blades are somewhat more forgiving of this treatment because the alloys usually added mitigate some of the effects of heat stress. However, a carbon-steel blade will not tolerate the temperature extremes. Both for the time it takes and for the risk involved, it is a good idea to grind as little as possible.

GRINDING EQUIPMENT

At some point, you will have to reshape a blade edge. For this reason, some sort of grinding device is indispensable. The power-grinding wheel is the most common, and probably, all things considered, the most practical. Get the slow-speed version (1,750rpm or so) and 8" (203mm) wheels for less undercutting of the edge. Keep the wheels trued and clean. Keep your finger behind the bevel, and work patiently.

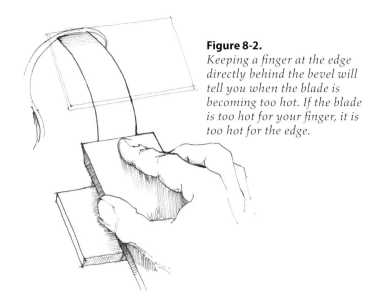

Figure 8-2.
Keeping a finger at the edge directly behind the bevel will tell you when the blade is becoming too hot. If the blade is too hot for your finger, it is too hot for the edge.

GRINDING OUT A NICK

Do not remove a nick by grinding the bevel; grind perpendicular to the edge. After removing the nick, grind the bevel until it just reaches the edge. If you grind out the nick by grinding the bevel, you are always working at the thin edge. This thin edge has no mass to help dissipate the heat, and is therefore at greater risk for overheating.

An alternative to the grinding wheel is the standing stationary belt sander, about 2" (51mm) wide. Knife makers and many metalworkers prefer them. These sanders cut aggressively but have less tendency to overheat because the sanding belt carries away much of the heat. (You still can be too aggressive and overheat the blade, but it is much harder to do than with a grinding wheel). This machine allows you several options for shaping the bevel. Besides the flat platen that produces a (nearly) flat bevel, usually you can work at one of the end wheels of the belt and achieve a hollow grind. The machine I have has an 8" (203mm) wheel that is usable. In addition, most machines have an arbor at the other side of

GRINDING ON A SANDING BELT

The natural tendency of a sanding belt is to round the pieces being sanded at both the approach to and exit from the piece. Reshaping the platen to give it a slight convexity compensates somewhat, reducing rounding at the approach and exit. Any remaining deviation from flat is little enough to easily remove when honing.

Alternatively, a partial hollow can be established within a few seconds by putting the blade on the end wheel (in which case you will need a tool rest there as well), just enough to establish good registration on the stones and speed honing to the edge.

the motor, which can be fitted with a grinding or buffing wheel.

Water grinding stones guarantee no heating of the edge. They tend to be slower (though not much) than power grinding or sanding, but they leave a great edge with little risk to the blade. They are in some respects less versatile. You cannot do general reshaping tasks, such as grinding a new blade profile (as for a molding plane). On the other hand, the horizontal water grinder can sharpen power jointer and plane blades, something other grinders cannot easily do. Also, the horizontal wheel leaves a dead flat bevel, which no other grinding wheel does. It does need more maintenance than the others, though. The stones quickly wear and require frequent truing.

There are also horizontal dry grinders made especially for woodworking tools. These look like they have several advantages, but

I have not worked with them. I'll leave it to the woodworking magazine reviews for more information on these.

Vertical water grinding wheels have the same advantage as the horizontal water wheels. There is no risk of heat damage to the tool, but they leave a hollow grind. It is a matter of preference as to what shape you want behind your edge. Most of the wheels are much larger than most dry grinding wheels, so edges are undercut less. In addition, some of the systems seem quite elaborate—and expensive—and, considering you will probably have to get another system for the shop's other grinding/shaping tasks, the cost seems downright luxurious.

Sharpening Stones

It was not that long ago that woodworkers did not have many options for honing the edges on blades. Oilstones or Arkansas stones were pretty much it. Oilstones were messy. They still clogged with debris, decreasing their effectiveness, despite all of the oil that was supposed to float away the debris. In addition, flattening them was impossible, and they did not cut very fast. Arkansas stones, a natural stone, were a step up, but the quality of the stones varied widely, and they shared many of the problems of the oilstones.

In the 1970s, manufactured Japanese waterstones became available, and they have revolutionized sharpening. Since then, major strides have been made in the quality and type of product available. American manufacturers now make waterstones, and by reports, their product is equal to, if not better than, some Japanese stones. I cannot keep track of all of the different stones. I have settled on a number of stones that serve my needs, so I have not experimented widely with the different ones available. I suggest you consult the woodworking magazine reviews for comparisons of products and systems.

Nevertheless, you have to take some of the tests they do with a grain of salt. It is not simply a matter of which is the best sharpening stone, or the best sharpening system, but the best match, blade to stone. Though I have no verification for this, I suspect the technique used also is a factor in the effectiveness of different sharpening stones. I would not lose sleep at night over matching stone to blade, but some broad categories can be delineated. The clearest distinction can be made between the alloy steels and the carbon steels. Waterstones are much less effective on many of the alloy steels. On some alloys, waterstones do not really cut at all. If your waterstones seem ineffective on your alloy blades, you will have to use diamond stones and/or paste.

After that, determinations become much more subtle. When first imported, Japanese waterstones reflected the unique characteristics of the Japanese blade. Now they are responding more to the American market. The Japanese

DIAMOND STONES

Diamond stones actually cut faster and smoother as they wear. This is because, at least in the polycrystalline stones, the large points break into many smaller points, creating both a finer cut and more points to more quickly abrade the surface.

craftsman, intimately familiar with the character of his tools, will prefer different stones for different tools, because he knows that certain matches yield better results. The common Western carbon-steel blade is not very subtle or complex. A 1,200-grit stone followed by a 4,000-grit polishing stone often gives you as good a result as more time spent on finer stones. Laminated blades, both Japanese and cast steel, generally respond well to an additional polishing stone, 6,000- to 8,000-grit, using a 3,000-grit stone as an intermediate.

OTHER ABRASIVES

A few other sharpening materials can be useful. I have mentioned diamond stones. These are particularly useful for flattening the back of blades, as you can hone on them almost indefinitely without wearing them out of flat. With a waterstone, if your blade back needs a lot of flattening, the waterstone soon wears out of flat and will have to be flattened again. If you wait too long to do it, the curve of the stone will be honed into the back of the blade, so using a non-wearing "stone" is helpful here (Figure 8-3, 8-4, and 8-5).

If your plane blade back is badly out of flat, it may be faster to use carborundum

STONE CHOICES

I use a #1200 Bester ceramic waterstone, an Aoto Mountain Blue Stone (about #3000), and a North Mountain Super Polish Stone (about #8000). I recently purchased a natural finish stone (#4 grade, all I could afford) for my best Japanese plane blades. If you are just starting out, I would suggest a #1000 or #1200 ceramic waterstone, such as the Bester, and a #4000 or possibly #6000 finish stone.

Figure 8-3. *Besides using a straight edge to check the stones for flat (which I find difficult when the stones are wet), you can check by using your flattening stone, which in this case is a diamond stone. A few strokes with the flattening stone will reveal the hollow, stained with the iron removed in sharpening.*

Figure 8-4. *Here the stone is almost restored to flat.*

Figure 8-5. *Flat once again.*

USING AND MAINTAINING WATERSTONES

Before use, synthetic waterstones need to be soaked for at least ten minutes, or until air bubbles stop coming out of the stone. If they do not have a wood base, you can store them indefinitely in water. A large lidded plastic tub is good for this. If they have a wooden base, you can still store them in water, but eventually the base will fall off. Synthetic finish stones (#3000 and above) generally do not need to be soaked, but check with the manufacture and/or dealer.

Natural waterstones are never stored in water because doing so causes them to disintegrate. Coarser stones are soaked for 5 or 10 minutes before using and removed after sharpening. The natural finish stones generally do not need to be soaked, but again check with the seller. Natural stones will often crack if they are allowed to freeze, whether dry or in water.

The stones will have to be trued before they are used the first time and frequently as they are used. There are a number of ways to do this. My favored approach now is to use a diamond stone rubbed against the waterstone. I have been using the same diamond stone now for more than eight years and it has not worn out yet, so it is cost effective. Alternatively, you can use sandpaper—220-grit wet/dry on a piece of ¼" (6mm) plate glass laid on a flat surface.

However, you will get only about two flattenings before the sandpaper wears out, so costs can add up. In addition, sandpaper tends to glaze some stones (such as the Bester), so it is not always an option. I have also flattened stones on a concrete block, which works fine until the concrete becomes polished and the block wears out of flat. Also, a special stone is sold just for flattening sharpening stones, which works fine, but eventually it too gets glazed and out of flat.

Some stones are harder than others, so the frequency of flattening will vary. Frequency also varies according to the task. A good procedure is to sharpen your finest smoothing plane blade first, right after flattening the stones. Then follow in order with blades of increasing edge curvature, right down to the jack. That way you can actually use the wear of the stones to help shape the blade edges. You can even set aside old badly worn stones to hone blades of significant curvature (like a scrub-plane blade).

In use, coarser stones are periodically washed clean and kept wet by adding a bit of water from the soaking container. The blade is abraded directly against the stone. The finish stones are kept barely wet, but not allowed to dry out; the slurry is allowed to build up, as this is what actually does the polishing, not direct contact with the stone. Using a *nagura* stone (a chalk stone available where waterstones are sold) raises the slurry more quickly.

on an iron plate *(kanaban)* to flatten it. The iron grabs the carborundum and keeps it from grinding the plate, though it will wear out eventually and have to be replaced (see "Flattening the Back of a Plane Blade" on page 97).

A hard felt wheel can be useful. It must be hard felt to minimize rounding over of the edge. While I would never use this on my good smoothing-plane blades, it is sometimes helpful to touch up the blade on a jack or scrub plane. Felt wheels often cut faster than you think, so it is easy to distort—or even slightly gouge—a subtle, critical edge. This slight distortion and the very slight rounding that result from using a hard felt wheel is less critical to the blade of a plane used for dimensioning or shaping. The back must still be lapped on the finish stone. Eventually, buffing will round the bevel of the blade. It must then be hollow ground, at least partially, and stoned to a good edge to keep the blade cutting effectively, before it approaches the buffing wheel again.

Technique

I learned to sharpen on the floor. It has a number of advantages: You do not need to build a special table and have it take up space in your shop, and sitting, kneeling, or squatting can actually be restful to legs that have been standing all day. However, I do not seriously believe I can convince many people reading this to even try it, though I do highly recommend it.

What I learned from using this position is that it is of little importance whether you are on the floor, sitting, or standing. What is important is the height of the stone relative to the body, and a solid, centered position that allows for both movement and stability. The stone should be about 4" or 5" (102mm or 127mm) below the belly button. Lower than this and your will overextend your arms at the end of the stroke. Any higher and your elbows will be too bent and flailing about. Both positions will cause you to rock the blade on its bevel, rounding it over. Even if you use a jig, this is a good position, because it maximizes the energy of your movement.

Position yourself to maintain good, solid

LISTENING

Learn to recognize the sound of the full bevel being stroked on the stone: whenever the blade is rocked or lifted, the pitch of this sound of the blade on the stone will change. It will sound different when just the heel of the bevel is stroked, and different again when just the edge is stroked. In fact, there is a slight bit of difference in sound when pressure is applied more toward the edge than the heel—even though the blade is sitting flat on the stone.

Responding to the feedback that sound gives you is an important lesson that will carry throughout all your work. It can tell you when you are nearing the end of the cut with a handsaw even though you can't see it, when a power tool needs to be turned off—immediately—and investigated for a dangerous problem, and when you have just lifted the blade off its bevel and are starting to cause problems for yourself.

balance even at the extremes of each stroke. If standing, have your feet apart, one slightly in front of the other. Feel the bevel lying flat on the stone and learn to recognize the feel and sound when the bevel loses full contact with the stone and rocks. Stop and feel the bevel's position again. Train your body to follow the bevel, to internalize the movement required to keep that bevel flat to the stone, and to maximize the expenditure of energy directly to the cutting edge itself. Have your mind focused on this cutting edge and this bevel in solid contact with the stone, with the body following in total attention and coordination. This is the beginning of skill.

SHARPENING

Years ago, a young man apprenticed to a furniture maker in Japan showed me this sharpening technique. It has served me well. I suspect it will do likewise for you

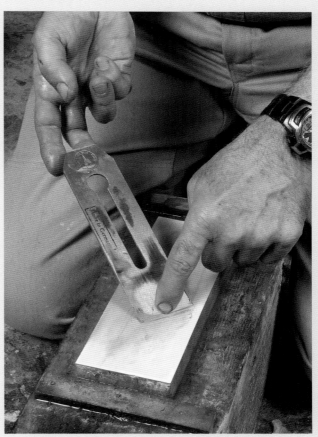

Figure 1. *Before beginning to sharpen, first find the bevel. You do this by putting one or two fingers down on top of the blade directly opposite the bevel, while simultaneously tilting the blade up with a single finger of the other hand underneath. Tilt the blade up and down with this finger while keeping pressure down on the bevel with the other hand until you can feel the blade rest securely on the flat of the bevel. Do this exercise every time before you start sharpening, and several times during.*

SHARPENING *(continued)*

Figure 2. *Similar to the exercise, when sharpening, the first one or two fingers of the off hand—the left if you're right-handed—finds and maintains a steady pressure down on the bevel. At the same time, the right hand lightly grips the blade with the thumb and second finger, maintaining the angle, with the first finger applying downward pressure on the bevel (along with those of the left hand). The third and fourth fingers are lightly wrapped underneath. The number of fingers in each position may vary as sharpening proceeds, but the basic positions of the first fingers of each hand putting pressure on the bevel with the rest of the fingers of the right hand maintaining angle of the blade remain the same. With the longer Western blade, the hand must wrap over the top of the blade. This makes the correct height of the sharpening stones especially important, as a too-high position will result in an awkward turning of the wrist when sharpening. These blades are also trickier as they are thinner and the bevel gives less of a support base, and the long blade makes it easy to lever it out of the correct angle.*

When moving the blade back and forth over the stone, the finger(s) of the left hand maintain a constant pressure down on the bevel to make sure it stays in constant contact with the stone. The right hand generally does the moving, assisted by the left hand, though neither hand does only one task: they each assist the other.

Listen to and feel the bevel: when you sense you are no longer holding the bevel in constant contact with the stone—stop, relax your hands, do the exercise of finding the bevel, and start again.

Special Note: Do not attempt to steady the blade by putting fingers on the stone and dragging them along as you sharpen. This will soon cut through your fingertips, though you will not feel it until after it has happened, resulting in a painful, slow-to-heal wound.

Once you have had some practice sharpening and have gotten a better feel for keeping the bevel, you can begin working on an advanced technique. This is to actually put the focus of the sharpening effort right at the edge while still keeping the bevel flat on the stone when sharpening. It took me a while to discover this: after I got proficient at keeping the bevel flat, I noticed that over time the bevel angle on my laminated blades was getting smaller. I finally figured out that because the edge steel is harder than the backing steel, equal pressure across the bevel will wear away the softer

Figure 3. *The back of the blade is lapped with a similar grip and pressure distribution as when doing the bevel: the right hands grips the blade with the thumb and second finger, with the first finger putting pressure on the very edge of the blade. The fingers of the left hand also put pressure just at the blade's edge. While the blade is never, ever lifted, the right hand does contribute an upward pressure at the off end of the blade while simultaneously focusing pressure down at the edge. The blade, of course, stays in solid contact with the stone the whole time.*

steel more quickly, eventually making the bevel angle smaller.

To compensate, I concentrated my pressure on the edge itself, while still keeping the bevel flat to the stones. Blades suddenly became sharper a lot faster. To do this, the right hand that supports the blade gives a little bit of pressure—focus—on the cutting edge itself by increasing the support it gives underneath the end of the blade while simultaneously concentrating the front fingers on the edge. I could say something like "the right hand lifts the end of the blade imperceptibly" instead to describe this, but this would give the wrong impression: it is an upward pressure there coupled with focused pressure at the blade's edge (rather than just the bevel). The blade is never actually lifted because this would round the bevel.

The required bit of curvature can be put on a smoothing plane blade by alternately putting pressure on each corner of the blade with the fingers that reside above the bevel. This is done three or four strokes at a time, on each stone. Similarly, pay attention to the distribution of pressure with the fingers. Unequal pressure may result in an unexpected and unwanted blade shape.

9

BENCH WORK
Of Slaves, Dogs, and Deadmen

Over many generations, European cabinetmakers developed a very sophisticated bench for

holding work that was to be planed and joined. This bench, especially when used along with

its various accessories, will hold pieces of almost any shape in virtually any of the positions

that might be required to effectively work them: shaping, dimensioning, smoothing, joining,

whatever. If you work in a variety of styles, especially in the traditional styles, you will

eventually have to invest in this classic bench, or one like it.

This large board is held in the front vise and supported on pegs set into the face of the bench's legs while its edge is planed. The ability to hold work securely, and position it quickly, greatly increases productivity.

While there are numerous variations of the European bench, they all have at least one distinguishing feature: a row of dog holes—traditionally square, sometimes round in contemporary versions—into which adjustable height pegs, or *dogs,* are put. Used with a *tail vise* on the end of the bench, the dogs run the length of the bench at regular intervals near the front edge. The tail vise also has one or more dog holes, allowing the user to clamp a length of board between a dog in the bench and a dog in the end vise when the vise is tightened. This innovation allows a variety of shapes and sizes of boards and panels to be fastened securely while they are being planed or otherwise worked, a very helpful feature.

The bench also typically has a vise on the front (at the opposite end of the bench from the tail vise) that is used to hold work for almost everything else that must be done, as well as for holding smaller pieces when planing. This front vise has a number of variations depending largely on the type of furniture being made and the bench's region of origin and each has its advantages and drawbacks. The leg vise, one of the oldest forms of vises, can hold a variety of sizes and a limited amount of shapes, but is cumbersome to readjust while working, though some new versions are improving on this.

The shoulder vise, which has the clamping face mounted to the screw with a swivel fitting, can clamp a variety of straight and tapered pieces, but can get in the way when working edges on long pieces. The classic woodworking vise we're all familiar with can have a quick-adjustment mechanism, making it easy to go back and forth between large and small pieces quickly, but cannot easily hold tapered or odd-shaped pieces. An Emmert-style vise, designed for use by patternmakers, can hold just about anything, in a lot of different positions, though it can require some jigging if, for instance, you want to shoot the edge of a long piece.

The only drawback I find to the classic European bench is that it can be a bit cumbersome or slow when you have to plane regularly shaped pieces, especially when you have many of them to do. On medium to small pieces, the time it takes to dog and un-dog a workpiece is roughly equal to the time it takes to plane a side. Thus, using the bench can double your work time.

Our predecessors noticed the problem. Specialty trades, for instance, often used much simpler benches and holding devices where work could be rapidly repositioned, with fresh pieces quickly replacing the finished ones. Craftsmen often worked by the piece, so speed was of the essence. If you did not have to take the time to turn a crank or vise handle to hold a piece and then turn it again to release it, you were saving time and energy, and making more money. Many of the trades were compensated barely above subsistence as it was.

A SIMPLE-STOP BENCH

The vast majority of pieces the woodworker will want to smooth with his plane can be worked against a simple stop affixed to the bench. Although bench dogs and vises of the European bench are useful for holding workpieces while chiseling or shaping as well as planing, it is often not necessary to clamp regular-shaped pieces down to the bench with dogs or other clamping devices just to plane them. A workpiece can have its first side smoothed (if it is small, a side can be smoothed in a pass or two), flipped end for end (to maintain the best grain orientation), planed, then turned onto its side and planed, and then flipped again end for end—all without having to reach for a vise handle. You can smooth a stack of parts quickly this way.

For planing, and even for much basic woodwork, you really do not need an elaborate bench. A stout plank with a stop affixed to it often will be the fastest and most effective way to hold the work. This stop should be as wide as possible, not a single iron or wood peg, in order to handle boards of various widths without the push of the plane causing the board to pivot away from you. The stop should preferably be a strip of wood fitted near the end of the planing board in a tapered dado or sliding dovetail so it can be removed or replaced.

A simple planing board, used with a holdfast and a few vise-type accessories, will be quite serviceable, and portable, and will probably serve the woodworker's planing and hand tool work quite well. If you have a European-style bench, however, there are a number of things you can do to speed planing operations.

ADDING VERSATILITY

To avoid having to repeatedly dog and un-dog boards you want to surface-plane, or having to install a fixed stop to work against on your bench, you can simply clamp a short board in the tail vise so it projects above the bench top and plane against it. This works best, of course, for short pieces. A device can be made for the front vise of only two pieces of wood to plane longer pieces (Figure 9-1).

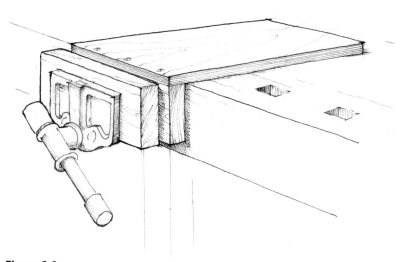

Figure 9-1.
For push planes, this simple planing stop clamps in the front vise. The top piece is ½" (13mm) thick or less. The block clamped in the vise is preferably solid wood ¾" (19mm) thick or thicker.

A SIMPLE BENCH

Years ago, in the basement of a house I was renting, I came across a 4x10 (102mm x 254mm) beam in amongst some scrap lumber, abandoned by the previous tenant. It was 8' long, had a series of pairs of ⁵⁄₁₆" (8mm) holes drilled through the broad face down its length, and a ledger screwed along the whole length of one edge. Obviously, someone had intended this to be a workbench, perhaps in the Japanese style. However, as it was, it did not appear that useable to me. Nevertheless, the wood was a nice piece of fir, dry and straight. I used it for years as a portable bench on the worksite, supporting it on a pair of workhorses, and gradually became aware of its potential (**Figure 1**).

I have since installed two removable stops of different heights at each end that slide in on tapered dovetails. They can be removed or moved to opposite ends as needed, with just a tap of the hammer. I need stops at either end because I use both push and pull planes (**Figure 2**).

I installed a wooden hook near one end above the ledger similar to the hook on the Roubo bench in Scott Landis's *The Workbench Book* (Taunton Press, 1987). This allows me to set a board on edge on the ledger and push the end of the board into the hook (again, without having to clamp or use a vise) to stabilize it while shooting the edge (**Figure 3**). The ledger along one side can also be used for shooting edges by setting the plane on the ledger with the board flat on the surface of the bench and using the bench as one large shooting board.

Into the holes, I inserted ⁵⁄₁₆" (8mm) dowels about an inch longer than the thickness of the bench. As it turned out, most fit snuggly, allowing me to adjust their height by tapping them up or down with a hammer. I generally do not use these as stops because they are rather small, but more for positioning alongside work to keep it from shifting to the side, because of either an irregular end or

Figure 1. *The planing bench in its simplest incarnation, sitting on a pair of workhorses (Japanese-style, in this case).*

Figure 2. *Full-width stops are fitted into dovetailed grooves near either end, so that they can be easily tapped out and removed or exchanged. Holes have been drilled for holdfasts.*

Figure 3. *This hook captures pieces for edge-planing when set on the ledger.*

Figure 4. *Clamp a handscrew to the bench for use as a versatile vise.*

Figure 5. *A chairmaker's vise can be clamped to the top.*

Figure 7. *I added a tool shelf behind the work surface and added a slotted stop against which I can work. In order to keep the horses from rocking from heavy planing, I pressure-fit a lower shelf on the stretchers of the horses to lock in their placement, pressure-fit the tool shelf, and added diagonal braces. Half-lapped and notched at either end to tightly fit to the top rail and stretchers of the horses, these help make the whole assembly rigid. Moreover, everything disassembles without tools.*

diagonal planing. If I had to do it over again I probably would make the holes ¾" (19mm) in diameter so dowels in them would be stout enough to use as stops, and then the holdfast could be used as well in the holes.

When I use the bench in the field, if I need to hold a piece for shaping or cutting, I clamp a large hand-screw clamp to the top at the end. This works quite well and, unlike many vises, will hold tapered pieces **(Figure 4).** If I really wanted a vise, I would probably fix it to the end rather than the face, so as to not interfere with the ledge on the front. In addition, for holding pieces to be shaped, a chairmaker's vise (sometimes called a carver's vise) could be clamped to the top through one of the holes drilled through it, allowing a variety of positions along the bench **(Figure 5).**

For some complex pieces and operations I still have to resort to my European bench, but for most planing operations I find this simple bench very versatile and much faster.

Figure 6. *The bench has seen adjustments and additions as I worked with it over time. I placed a couple of stout dowels in the bottom of the bench to fit into holes drilled into the workhorses to keep the bench from scooting around under heavy planing.*

Figure 8. *The planing bench at its home in the shop. When not being used in the field, the bench rests here atop my tool chests.*

For planing the edges of long, narrow pieces that will flex if not fully supported, I put a 4" (102mm) handscrew clamp in the tail vise (Figure 9-2). On the side of one of the jaws of the clamp, I have glued a strip of veneer (Figure 9-3). The veneer allows the other jaw to be adjusted freely when the clamp is held in the vise. When using the clamp, I first adjust it so the jaw opening matches the work it is holding. I position the clamp in the vise at a height that works with the piece I am planing (so it extends above the bench surface less than the thickness of the board being planed), tighten the tail vise to hold the clamp, and then the clamp to hold the piece.

DEADMEN AND HELPER BOYS

For planing the edges of long, wide pieces, you can use the front vise to hold pieces up to around 5' long if they are not so narrow to flex when planed. Longer pieces will have to be supported. There are a number of ways to do this. The first is to build a way into the bench. This assumes you are building your own bench or are willing to do some major modifications to an existing bench.

One way to increase the versatility of the European bench is to build the legs flush to the front edge of the bench and drill a series of ¾" (19mm) holes in the front right leg. This allows work up to about 3' wide (such as a door or tabletop) to be supported on edge, on a dowel or holdfast inserted into one of the holes. The left end clamps into the front vise and the right end rests on the dowel or holdfast. You can drill holes in the left leg as well, as shown on the next page, to aid in positioning large, heavy work before fixing it in the vise, but it is not necessary. This works

Figure 9-2. *A handscrew clamp in the tail vise is a versatile clamp for holding work to be planed.*

Figure 9-3. *Glue a piece of veneer to the side of one jaw to provide clearance that enables the other jaw to be moved while the clamp is in the vise.*

for pieces long enough to span from leg to leg.

For shorter pieces, some sort of helper (often known as a *deadman, slave,* or *helper boy*) is needed. If you are building your own bench, you can build two stretchers in the front, one low and one high, with runners on them to accommodate a traveling helper, similar to those found on Shaker benches. This is a board 6" to 8" (152mm to 203mm) wide with a series of staggered holes that slides back and forth on the stretchers (Figure 9-4). Some of the holes match the height of those you drilled into the legs. If you do not have the option (or energy) to build or rebuild the legs on your bench, a portable helper can be made, several designs for which exist (Figure 9-5).

Figure 9-4. *This European-style bench has peg holes in the legs and a traveling helper that rides on the top and bottom stretchers to help support long and wide pieces when edge-planing.*

BENCH DOGS

I have several recommendations for bench dogs. First, get rid of the metal ones that came with the bench. Sooner or later—and probably sooner—your plane blade will find them, often at high speed. Not only does this take enormous chunks out of the edge, but it damages the plane bottom as well. In addition, this assumes you do not simply set the plane down on one, nicking the blade or dinging the sole. In fact, remove all metal objects from the bench, including other tools, especially when planing, because they tend to knock into one another. Make new dogs out of wood; you can make lots of them and keep one in every hole to save time.

Figure 9-5. Bench Slave

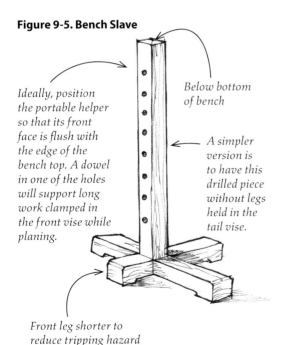

Ideally, position the portable helper so that its front face is flush with the edge of the bench top. A dowel in one of the holes will support long work clamped in the front vise while planing.

Below bottom of bench

A simpler version is to have this drilled piece without legs held in the tail vise.

Front leg shorter to reduce tripping hazard

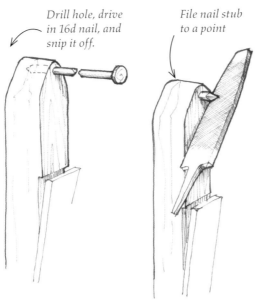

Drill hole, drive in 16d nail, and snip it off.

File nail stub to a point

Figure 9-6. Bench Dog with Tapered Head

A worthy variation on the bench dog is one that tapers and has a metal point fixed in its face (Figure 9-6). This is particularly useful for shaping or planing stock that must be rotated as it is worked. The safest variation has a 10d (or bigger) nail bedded in the face of it. Cut the nail off about ¼" (6mm) or so above the surface and file it to a point. If used frequently, the top of the dog will receive wear from the plane. With the metal point bedded only in the face, your plane does not find metal.

A faster way to make this dog is to drive a screw through the back until the point protrudes from the face. If the pieces you are planing are large and you use the dogs infrequently, these will probably serve as well, especially if you use a trim-head screw and countersink the head. I say probably, because, if you end up using the dogs a lot, you can end planing the top of the dog down over time and eventually knick your blade on the screw head.

Shooting an Edge

Planing a long edge to straighten it in preparation for gluing is called *shooting*. For most people it is one of the most frustrating tasks in woodworking. However, having a gentle curve honed into the edge of the blade of the jointer plane can make this task manageable. I like this technique better than others I have tried—and I think I have tried them all. If you are not too set in your ways already, try this one.

To plane an edge straight, you must have the focus of your attention and your energy at the cutting edge. The shaving (eventually) must emerge continuous, full width, and unbroken. At first, most of your energy will be everywhere but at the edge, causing tense muscles, cramped hands and shoulder and back muscles, and quick fatigue. Eventually, you will expend energy efficiently, with no muscles tensed except those used to cut the edge, and no wasted motion. You will be able to do this all day and feel better at the end of it than you would have if you had sat at a desk all day.

Practically speaking, the following things must be done: the stance must be balanced from the start to the finish of the stroke. The work must not be too high or too low. The planed edge at about 34" above the ground is good for a person 5' 8" to 5' 10" tall; less if you are shorter, more if you are taller. This will allow you to keep both your balance and your focus. The weight on the plane must be on the front at the start of the stroke and the

WINDING STICKS

Winding sticks can be any two sticks that are rectangular in section and long enough to lie across the work you are checking. The sticks need to be straight and have the two parallel edges. For checking timber, the sticks do not have to be of great refinement: you can literally grab two sticks out of the scrap pile—they don't even have to be the same width—as long as they are straight and parallel. The longer they are, the greater the accuracy in checking for parallel, as the greater length exaggerates the distortion.

If you want a tool of greater sophistication, you can buy wood or metal ones, or you can make your own. When making your own, the principal is simple enough. Pin two pieces of wood together so they can be separated, plane both edges straight, pull them apart, and check them by holding the edges together up to the light. Any error in straightness doubles. If light shines between the edges at any point, put them back together and plane them until no light is visible when they are held against one another. If the pieces are used in the same orientation as when they are pinned together (make a habit of doing this), it will make no difference, even if a taper has been planed along their length, because the pieces will still be parallel to one another **(Figure 1).**

To make a set of winding sticks, select two pieces of any stable, well dried wood, preferably quartersawn (mahogany is a good choice, as is white oak), say about 1½" (38mm) wide by ½" (13mm) thick by 18" (457mm) long. Align the two pieces, drill though both near the ends, and insert dowels through both. Glue the dowels to one side only so they can be pulled apart. It is helpful to relieve the inside edges of the ends so you can get your thumbs in to get them apart. Bevel the faces so the reference edges are about ⅛" (3mm) wide, in order to make them easier to read.

Figure 1. *A matched set of wood winding sticks.*

back at the finish, gradually shifting as the stroke progresses.

You can practice holding the front half of the plane at the beginning of the board edge using your left hand only, supporting the weight of the plane cantilevering off the back. Practice doing the same thing holding the back of the plane with your right hand only, supporting the cantilevered front of the plane off the far end of the board. Now practice smoothly shifting your weight while purposely lifting one hand and then the other as the stroke progresses. Every time your plane accidentally dips off the end at the start or the finish of a stroke, go back and practice this weight shift.

Learning to keep the plane in solid, continuous contact with the work will help you greatly in focusing on the cutting action of the plane. Keep your eyes on the throat of the plane, always monitoring the quality of the shaving that emerges.

TECHNIQUES FOR SHOOTING AN EDGE

1 One of the main difficulties in shooting an edge occurs when the edge is out of square. With a straight blade, you have to attempt to balance the plane square to the face, literally on the corner of the board, and plane that narrow edge repeatedly at the same angle.

2 You can, as I have seen recommended, clamp two boards together so that even though they are out of square with their faces, they will have the same angle. The boards are then flipped to be joined and their complementary angles zero each other out. There are two big problems with this method:

3 The first problem is that any error in the straightness will be doubled when the boards are joined. To correct the problem, the boards must be unclamped and checked and re-clamped and planed, and unclamped and checked, maybe many more times. The second problem is that the boards have to be perfectly realigned every time they are re-clamped, or the method will not work at all. This is tedious and time-consuming.

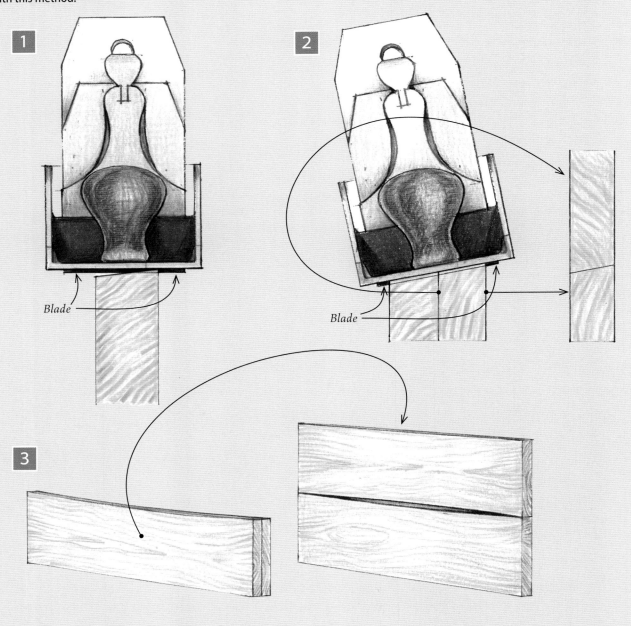

Blade

Blade

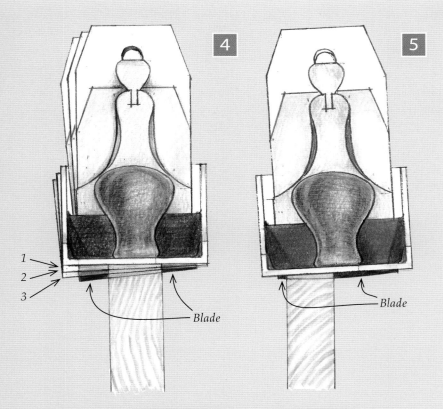

1
2
3

— Blade

— Blade

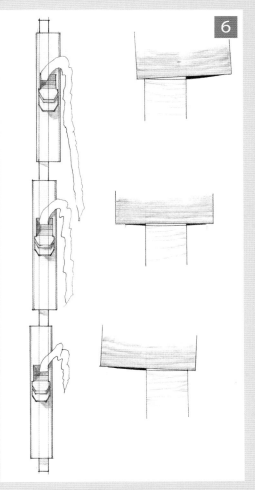

4 You can plane one board at a time, marking them to be flipped after planing so the angle of their edges will be complementary when joined, resulting in a flat panel. While you may find you favor one side or another repeatedly, this technique works consistently only when a shooting board is used. This is because with a shooting board the plane is referenced off its side so the angle planed onto the edge of the board will be consistent from board to board (as long as the blade is not readjusted). Without a shooting board, even if you repeatedly favor one side, this technique has problems. If your plane's straight blade is out of parallel with the sole of the plane, each stroke will increase the error. If you plane one board's edge more than the other, then your angles will not match, and you are back to where we started—correcting the angle on the edge of the board, trying to balance the plane.

5 If you have a bit of a curve to the edge of your 2¾" (70mm)-wide jointer-plane blade, set the sole of the plane flat on the edge. You will not have to balance it and by keeping the plane so that the board is to one side of it or another, you can alter and correct the angle in one or a few strokes. Traditionally, the edge of the jointer-plane blade was sharpened to a curve projecting as much as ¹⁄₃₂" (0.8mm) because the plane was used to smooth out the scallops of the jack plane as well as shoot edges. Nowadays, the jointer is used principally to shoot edges, and while this much blade curvature may present a useful amount of concavity on the edge of a ¾" (19mm) board, it may be a little much on thicker boards. I have been sharpening my blades so that they project about ¹⁄₆₄" (0.4mm) over the 2¾" (70mm) width of the blade (which, because of the blade's bedded angle to the sole, is about ¹⁄₃₂" (0.8mm) of curvature on the blade itself). I find this amount of curve very serviceable.

6 Because using the plane to one side of the board or the other effectively lowers that side, you can even take out a twist in the edge by starting the plane with the board to one side of the plane and finishing with the board on the other. After you have checked for square, make a pass down the board with the plane centered on the edge, repeating until a continuous unbroken full-width shaving emerges, indicating that your edge is now a flat continuous plane.

10

MAKING & USING SHOOTING BOARDS

Invaluable, Often-Overlooked Tools

The stop of this shooting board prevents the end grain of the tenon's shoulder from splitting out as the shoulder plane exits the cut.

Probably the single most effective accessory for any bench is the shooting board, or its cousin, the bench hook (Figure 10-1). I underestimated the usefulness of this tool for a long time but have gradually become more and more appreciative of its speed and versatility. Its first use is the trimming of ends of pieces with a plane, either square (probably most useful) or at a particular angle, such as 45°, done on a shooting board made just for this angle. Using a shooting board for trimming can greatly increase your accuracy. You can take off the thickness of a shaving, say a few thousandths of an inch with each stroke, giving you incredible accuracy, and because the stop supports the grain at the back of the strip, you do not have to worry about your piece chipping out at the exit side of the cut.

Did you ever have to trim the length of a piece to fit precisely between two others, such as a panel stop or a frame rail? You carefully make your mark and cut it on the chop saw or table saw, probably a little conservatively. Chances are it is a bit tight. You go back over to the power saw and try to cut that whisker of thickness off. You walk back to the cabinet or frame you are working on and try it. You walk back to the saw again and try to cut just a whisker off. You walk back to the work and try it again. You do it repeatedly, with more or less success, with a multitude of pieces. The process is time consuming and rather frustrating. It is difficult to cut just a few thousandths of an inch off using a power saw to get that exact fit, and on small pieces, it can be downright dangerous. You ultimately

settled for a fit that was not quite as good as you would have liked.

With the shooting board, you can take the board right to where the work needs to be fit. If the piece to be cut is small, you can mark and cut the piece with a handsaw and clean it up with a plane, all right there on the shooting board. Take a few thousandths off with a stroke of the plane and check it. Another stroke or three, check, and you are finished. There is no walking back and forth across the shop, and the piece drops in with an airtight fit. The process is fast and accurate. It works particularly well for fitting drawer parts, where the back, sides, and front can all be sized, to both length and width, exactly to

Figure 10-1. *Three variations of the shooting board. Left: the sloping ramp extends the wear from cutting thin material over a wider area of the plane blade. Center, the parallel ramp will shoot thicker stock. Both these boards have stops fixed with a sliding dovetail. The shooting board on the right is the down-and-dirty version, with a piece of ¼" (6mm) hardboard creating the ramp and screwed-on stops.*

fit the pocket for which they are being made. And, if the bench stop on the underside of the shooting board is cut down to ⅜" (10mm) thick or so, flip it and plane the faces of the drawer parts as well using that simple stop to plane against, again speeding the work.

When smoothing ends of boards with a plane without a shooting board, you will have to do one of two things to keep the ends of the cut from splintering out: you will have to back up the cut when making a stroke the full width of the board, or you will have to plane in from either side.

In the first instance, you can put the board in a vise and clamp a block of wood the same thickness to one side of the board to restrain the grain from splintering. I personally find this tedious and slow going, and oftentimes the board is too long to be stood up in the vise and must be put at some awkward angle. It also does not guarantee that the end will be square, either to the sides or to the face.

Planing in from both ends (the second method) tends to leave a slight hump in the middle where the plane strokes meet, though this can be avoided with care. It also leaves a different pattern on the end grain from the two different planing directions, which takes more sanding to remove than when the end grain is planed from a single direction. Again, it does not guarantee that the end will be square.

The most expeditious method to smoothing the ends of a board is to use a shooting board. You can plane the end of a board completely from one direction, avoiding irregularities. The stop you plane against keeps the side

BENCH HOOK VERSUS SHOOTING BOARD

A bench hook is almost identical to the shooting board. The differences are that the bench hook does not have a ramp (also called a ledge, or rebate), it tends to be shorter than a shooting board, and it is used mostly as a saw stop, though it can also be used for shooting edges and ends. The shooting board usually has a ramp, can be as long as needed when used to shoot edges, and is primarily used for planing ends and edges, though it, as well, can be used as a saw stop.

from splintering out. You do not have to do any tedious clamping. You are not limited in the length of board you can work on. Your width is only limited by the size of the shooting board you have. While it does take some user input, the shooting board almost guarantees a square and straight end (Figure 10-2).

A shooting board made at a 45° angle is also useful—indispensable, really—if you are doing miters such as the ends of stops for holding panels or glass within the stiles and rails of a door. A shooting board for 45° trimming was my first shooting board,

Figure 10-2. *A shooting board solves all the problems of planing an end-grain edge. You can quickly and easily plane virtually any size board, producing a perfectly straight, square, splinter-free, and consistent-looking edge, not to mention continuous transparent shavings—but only if the plane is properly sharpened and set.*

actually. Years ago, I was trying to fit many stops on several glass doors for a cabinet. Despite setting up consistent jigs for cutting the different lengths, quite a number of the stops still needed finessing, resulting in much frustration and lost time.

Later, I mentioned this problem to my uncle, who was a patternmaker, and he sent back a drawing of a shooting board for trimming miters, a device he had used for years. The drawing was enlightening (Figure 10-3). This tool makes trimming pieces to

Figure 10-3.
A 45° shooting board is indispensable for fine miter work.

Figure 10-4. Shooting Board for Miters
(Construction similar to Figure 10-7 Quick and Easy Shooting Board on page 162).

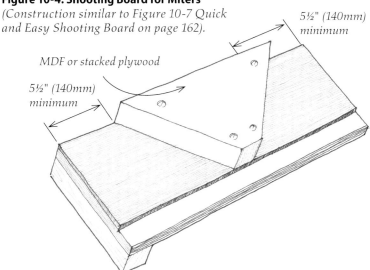

MDF or stacked plywood

5½" (140mm) minimum

5½" (140mm) minimum

exact length easy and safe, and can be built for trimming at any angle. They are often worth making at that angle if you have many joints to trim (Figure 10-4).

Another joint that often needs trimming is the face miter, that is, a miter cut across the width of the board at the end of a 1x4 or 1x6, for instance, as might be found in a fascia or baseboard of a cabinet. This mitered end is wider than the plane blade and thus can't be used with the shooting board previously described. Traditionally, variations of a device often called a donkey's ear, miter jack, or miter shooting block were used to help shoot this joint. These always looked to me to be awkward to use, elaborate to make, and expensive to buy—when you could find them.

When using the donkey's ear, because the work is held at an angle to the floor, the length of the piece to be trimmed is limited by the working height off the floor. Eventually, I figured out a simplified version of the traditional shooting board to trim these miters (Figure 10-5). Moreover, because it functions similarly to the classic shooting board, the length of the piece to be trimmed is not limited. Basically, it is a shooting board with the ledge at 45° to the surface upon which the work rests. The edge of this surface and the stop are cut at a complementary 45° to back up the plane cut (Figure 10-6).

You can use any plane on a shooting board, except a rabbet plane, as a rabbet plane will continually cut into the ledge on which it rides. Lower-angle planes—ones with a 45° cutting (blade) angle or less—will work

Figure 10-5. *This shooting board is for trimming face miters: a 45° angle cut across the grain of wide boards.*

Figure 10-6. Shooting Board for Face Miters
(Construction is similar to shooting board (Figure 10-5, above.)

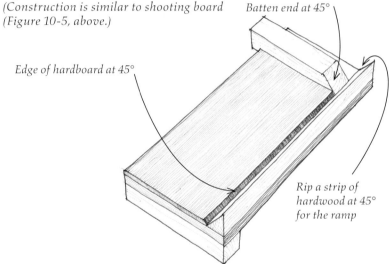

Batten end at 45°

Edge of hardboard at 45°

Rip a strip of hardwood at 45° for the ramp

made an iron version of this plane, the #51 that went with its own iron shooting/miter board, called the #52. Recently Lie-Nielsen has reproduced the #51 and has plans to produce the #52; and Lee Valley has brought out a re-engineered, bevel-up version of the #51 as well as a miter plane. Before World War II it was not uncommon to see the #51/#52 in the larger shops. It does a beautiful job—but is not really necessary for an effective shooting board.

Heft or extra length is not necessary in a plane used on the shooting board. The main requirements are:
- Keep the blade sharp—and sharpened straight with no curve and adjusted parallel to the sole
- Square the sole to the side that runs on the ledge
- Use a light cut with the plane

In use, the plane blade touches the workpiece and the user pushes it the length of the cut to shear a shaving off. Many first-time users make the mistake of having the blade adjusted too far out, causing the plane to stall in the cut.

The common reaction is to get a running start with the plane and crash it into the piece. Don't. It is hard on the plane (and you) and results in inaccurate work. Adjust the plane for a light cut. If the plane does not seem to be cutting, make sure the end of the piece is projecting a fraction past the stop. The plane may cut only a tiny piece of the corner at first, but will gradually extend the cut. You should be able to shear the shaving off in a smooth push. Admittedly, however,

better for cutting end grain. The low-angle Stanley-style block plane is a good candidate, although many woodworkers prefer one of the larger bench planes. The low-angle jack and smoothing planes are also good choices. In addition, some planes were made specifically for miter or shooting-board work (called, coincidentally, *miter planes*). And a special wooden plane was sometimes used, fitted with an iron plate at the throat for wear, a skewed blade for a shearing cut, and a handle to hook your hand around mounted at an angle to the work. At one time Stanley

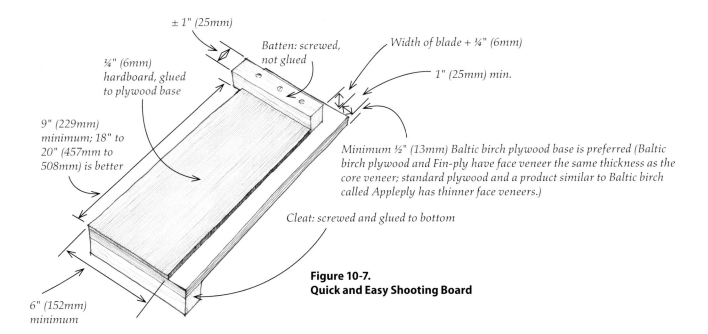

± 1" (25mm)

¼" (6mm)
hardboard, glued
to plywood base

Batten: screwed,
not glued

Width of blade + ¼" (6mm)

1" (25mm) min.

9" (229mm)
minimum; 18" to
20" (457mm to
508mm) is better

Minimum ½" (13mm) Baltic birch plywood base is preferred (Baltic
birch plywood and Fin-ply have face veneer the same thickness as the
core veneer; standard plywood and a product similar to Baltic birch
called Appleply has thinner face veneers.)

Cleat: screwed and glued to bottom

**Figure 10-7.
Quick and Easy Shooting Board**

6" (152mm)
minimum

some cuts will require a bit of momentum.

On a shooting board, the piece to be planed
is restrained by a stop that also supports the
back edge of the end of the piece, keeping
it from chipping out (Figure 10-7). The end
of this stop can, over time, get worn back,
reducing its chip-restraining ability. Also,
over time, sometimes the stop shifts its
alignment slightly, requiring readjustment.
For these reasons, it is a good idea to make
the stop replaceable.

In order to solve the (rather minor)
problem of having to periodically renew
the stop, I've fabricated a shooting board
that uses a stop that is fixed to the board
with a tapering, single-sided sliding dovetail
friction-fit into place. This piece has extra
length so it can be removed, the working end
renewed, and the stop tapped back into place.
In order to extend the wear across a wider
portion of the blade and the time between

sharpenings, and simultaneously reduce
blade wear on the one narrow portion of the
blade that happens as a result of a running
of the plane on a parallel ledge (especially
with thin stock), I cut the ledge as a long
tapering rabbet, creating a ramp for the plane
to ride on. None of this is necessary for a
shooting board to function well, but besides
looking better than a piece of hardboard on
your bench, it is a good project with which to
learn how to make tapering sliding dovetails.
Tapered sliding dovetail battens are very
useful in solid wood construction for keeping
wide panels such as doors and tabletops
flat. Additionally, the project is a good
demonstration of the use of a number of the
specialty planes.

INDEX